EMPOWER YOUR ASK

MODERN NEGOTIATION TACTICS FOR SELF-STARTERS, JOB SEEKERS, AND ENTREPRENEURS

JORDAN BLAKE

Copyright © 2025 BY Synast Publishing

Published by Synast Publishing

ISBN: 978-1-968418-39-7

INTRODUCTION

In today's rapidly evolving professional landscape, the ability to negotiate effectively has never been more crucial. Whether you're a self-starter carving out a niche in a competitive market, a job seeker vying for your dream position, or an entrepreneur striving to close deals and expand your enterprise, mastering the art of negotiation can be the key to unlocking unprecedented opportunities. Yet, many find themselves daunted by the prospect, often falling prey to common pitfalls such as feeling unprepared, misreading cues, or freezing in high-pressure moments.

This book sets out to demystify negotiation, presenting it not as an innate talent but as a learnable skill that anyone can acquire and refine. Drawing on a wealth of real-world scenarios, it offers practical, scenario-based tactics, ready-to-use scripts, and a suite of digital tools designed to equip you with the confidence and competence needed to excel in any negotiation setting. Whether you're dealing with aggressive counterparts or striving to secure win-win outcomes, the strategies within these pages are tailored for modern, hybrid work environments, ensuring relevance and applicability.

The content anticipates and addresses skepticism, acknowledging that many have traversed the negotiation literature landscape only to find themselves uninspired or unchanged. Here, the promise is distinct: actionable guidance that transcends industry boundaries, empowering even those who might not view themselves as natural negotiators. By fostering a mindset shift from zero-sum to win-win thinking, readers can learn to unlock creative deals and leverage mutual gain for better outcomes.

Through this journey, you'll learn to harness anxiety as a performance tool, transform conflict into opportunity, and build ethical leverage without aggression. The book provides a roadmap to negotiation mastery, covering essential aspects such as preparation, communication micro-skills, and psychological tactics. With this toolkit, you'll walk away with not only increased confidence and success rates but also stronger business relationships and a robust framework for continuous growth. Each chapter is crafted to engage, challenge, and inspire, prompting you to reflect on past negotiations and set intentions for future ones. Dive in and discover how every success can begin with an empowered ask.

Table of Contents

Chapter 1: Introduction to Empowered Negotiation

The Cost of Missed Opportunities

The burden of opportunities not taken can be significant and far-reaching in the context of negotiations. Such situations oftentimes set the course of careers and businesses, silently charting out the future by the utterance or the omission of the spoken word. The situation is unfortunately all too common: someone in the corporate world is on the fence, the ideal inquiry is not asked, and the opportunity of making a potentially great deal passes neglected or unnoticed, time and again.

Think through the less obvious and yet powerful differences in interactions during negotiation. These are not merely the making of offers and counteroffers but dances of timing, perception, and manoeuvre. In this, every moment of silence is a wayward vibe of what might have happened, and every lapse of time is a feeling of indecision that could as soon bend the outcome either toward or away. Stakes are high, and the price of no action can be high, usually in the form of lost revenues, reduced trends, and lost growth.

The psychology of missed opportunities can be in the fear of rejection or how uncomfortable it can be to enter the unknown. This psychological blockade can be even stronger than the potential profit of the inopportune absence of a certain question. There are numerous instances when professionals lose their voices when the most is needed; the multiplicity of possible failures overcomes them. Nonetheless, it is because of these junctures that the possibilities of an achievement are the highest.

In practical terms, the missed opportunity not only translates to a lost opportunity to make a deal but also may translate to a cascade of lost possibilities. As an example, one unasked question could spell the difference in establishing a long-term partnership and losing the client to a rival. This could fail to access important information, which could flip a negotiation to your advantage. The ripple effects of these omissions may go way beyond the immediate loss, creating an impact on future negotiations and the general credibility and reputation of the negotiator.

Furthermore, the fee that is paid in terms of lost opportunities is not monetary only. It can undermine trust, and as a result, professionals will find it more difficult to be assertive and straight to the point during further negotiations. The emotional cost may inflate a cycle that makes one hesitate; to each failure to act, the fear becomes more justified, and the fear of asking drives the hesitation cycle.

In order to eliminate such risks, a proactive attitude must be developed. This comes with vigorous training and adopting the attitude that no negotiation is a failure, but rather an opportunity to learn something new. By discarding any form of fear, a professional can turn a leap of faith into a leap of action. They will be able to learn how to detect the signals of hesitation and proactively do something about it, such that they not only spot potential opportunities but also go after them.

After all, the value of financial loss can be quite a lesson that it is strategically, rather than foolishly, to be prepared and ready to take chances. It points out the importance of the ability to arrive at the courage to ask, to engage, and explore the possibilities, however formidable they might be. By so doing, the negotiators not only increase their short-term results but also make themselves resilient to succeed in the future, giving potential losses the greatest of gains.

Common Negotiation Struggles

When working in the domain of negotiations, there is a list of typical pitfalls that can hinder the ability of the professional to achieve great results. These are not the obstacles at random but recurring themes that can spell discontinuation of any seasoned negotiator unless countered with foresight and deliberation. The key to breaking the cycle of such struggles is the realization that an understanding of these struggles is the key to triumphing over the struggle and making negotiation a powerful tool instead of a dreadful exercise.

One of the major obstacles in negotiation is the situation where one is not prepared. Most of them enter negotiations without a clear knowledge of their goals and targets and without a clear understanding of the goals and targets of the other party. Failure to prepare may easily lead to missed opportunities and allowances that would otherwise have been avoided. To counter this, prior to engaging in any negotiation, time should be invested in carrying out research and developing a strategy. This involves getting to know the needs, motivations, and areas where they might compromise both of the sides, which helps in fashioning a more informed and confident approach.

The other typical battle is locking up under pressure. Negotiations are often tense and stressful, causing some people to become stressed and not be able to react appropriately during the negotiations. It can be exacerbated by the fear of screwing up and being mistaken as one who is incompetent. Working on coping skills like breathing deeply, visualization, and rehearsal of worst-case scenarios can help a negotiator keep a cool head and think clearly.

Another common uphill in negotiations is misunderstanding signals. It is highly important to understand verbal and non-verbal signs well, as they may give true hints on what the other party plans and whether they are able to negotiate. Misunderstanding may cause misunderstanding and the loss of a possible compromise. In order to enhance this skill, negotiators need to pay attention to active listening and body language, as this can provide rich background information that cannot be conveyed by words alone.

There is also a challenge of confronting aggressive counterparts. Other parties can be quite intimidating in a negotiation, and this is one of the tactics they use to control the narrative. In situations like these, it is crucial to be calm and assertive, establish a clear line about what is and what is not acceptable, and make sure to steer the conversation away from personality and pitch it back on the matter of issues. Coming up with aggressive responses and rehearsal can enable him to attain control and shape the negotiation process into a more fruitful and respectful debate.

Last, the challenge to attain win-win solutions permeates negotiations. Some negotiators are trapped in a zero-sum situation, where the gains of one party are seen as the losses to the other. Such an attitude would not allow the search for creative alternatives that would be beneficial to all sides. The focus on joint efforts and win-win situations can shift negotiations to the creation of long-term beneficial relationships instead of a one-time situation.

After considering these issues commonly experienced in negotiation, professionals can increase their effectiveness and confidence when negotiating. Such precautionary measures reduce possible pitfalls in addition to creating an atmosphere that can lead to achieving successful and sustainable results.

Positioning Yourself as a Negotiator

The complex environment in negotiation means that one must first comprehend the many-faceted role of a negotiator. This goes beyond bargaining, and it entails the establishment of opportunity and the creation of relationships. A negotiator should be able to read the room and predict the unacknowledged needs and drivers of the various involved parties, as well as maneuver to get the desirable results.

Answers to the question of how to position oneself as a negotiator start with self-understanding. It is important to understand your wild cards and your hazard areas, as well as your advantages. This self-awareness enables you to play to your personal strengths and identify weak areas. Regardless of whether you are an introvert who excels with listening and preparation or an extrovert who is at ease building rapport and connection, the first task in customizing your negotiation style is to be aware of your instinctive style.

Besides self-awareness, in order to position oneself effectively, one needs to have a good understanding of one's context of negotiations. This involves knowing the critical participants, determining what is at stake, and being aware of the challenges and possible opportunities that would occur. The last thing that successful negotiators do is to walk into a negotiation without prior preparation; they equip themselves with information and knowledge that may prove to be a decisive point in negotiation. This involves carrying out investigations about the background, interest, and potential limitations of the other side, hence allowing the negotiator to come up with strategies on how to pursue his/her interest in a manner that the other party would be satisfied.

As an important element of positioning itself successfully, confidence can be viewed as a critical skill to be exercised. Confidence in negotiation is not about being argumentative or pushy; it is about portraying a peaceful confidence that is a result of proper preparation and having a clear direction. That confidence can be communicated by bodily language, intonation of words, and the artful silence. Silence as an under-recognized weapon of negotiation can prove to be a daunting weapon as it helps in ensuring that the negotiator remains in control, extracts a concession, or gets the other party to reveal more information.

Adequacy in terms of flexibility is another feature of a well-positioned negotiator. Although strict goals and limits should be set, flexibility also permits the negotiation professional to change direction when the circumstances require it, as new information comes to light or the negotiation environment shifts. This versatility is supported by a philosophy that does not think of win-lose outcomes where the negotiator is out to split the pie, but rather increase the size of the pie. With a mindset of mutual benefit, the negotiators are able to develop a long-term relationship that might go beyond a single transaction at hand.

Besides, a tactical negotiator is sensitive to the intricacies of speech. This concerns not only what is said but also the unsaid words. Active listening, the art of asking high-precision questions, and the capability to read between the lines will be needed to unravel the hidden interests and potential deal breakers. Such skills help the negotiator move easily through complex discourses and recognize the chances to use creativity in resolving the discussions.

Being a negotiator in the end is a combination of preparation, being able to adapt to situations, and interpersonal skills. It takes a commitment of continual learning and personal betterment, with each negotiation being a different test with its own multiple lessons to be learnt. By nurturing these elements, a negotiator can not only develop a reputation as an effective negotiator capable of negotiating good results, but also develop a reputation as someone who can be trusted as an effective negotiator in any situation.

The Promise of Empowered Negotiation

Empowerment in the field of negotiation can take place through both the results and the process. The bargaining process itself is a chance to re-imagine a communication style, decision-making, and connection. The chapter explores how, through the process of negotiation, individuals are able to use the strength of negotiation to transform their professional and personal interactions into places of empowerment.

The first step on the path to empowered negotiation is the desire to change the way of thinking and forget about the attitude connected to zero-sum, where the decrease of one party is a profit for the other side. Rather, it will adopt a win-win outcome that involves expanding the pie as opposed to slicing it. Such an attitude will help negotiators extend beyond short-term costs and benefits and seek to establish long-term value and relationships. In that way, they develop a more proactive and favorable attitude, which is necessary when it comes to the success of the negotiation results.

The crux of empowered negotiation is state and preparation. This entails not only knowing their own need and priorities but also the needs and interests of the other party. There is a well-developed preparation, without which negotiators can enter into the discussions filled with uncertainty and confusion. It also helps them find common ground and possible points of collaboration that are paramount in the making of mutually beneficial agreements.

The other pillar is effective communication. It demands effective listening, understanding, and being able to present one's needs and concerns clearly, and to do so confidently and assertively. Open and honest communications allow the negotiators to create trust and rapport, and it is the core issue in overcoming the obstacle and coming to an agreement. Also, learning how to ask high-precision questions may reveal secret intent and interest, which is insightful into the particular nature of the negotiation.

Managing emotions is proving to be one of the most effective weapons an empowered negotiator can have, whether working with his emotions or those of his partner. Emotional intelligence is extremely important when it comes to keeping composure and resilience in high-stress scenarios. By acknowledging and managing emotions, negotiators will be able to prevent conflicts from taking over and continuing the discussion on the matter. It can also be used to find ways to be more creative in problem-solving and compromise, allied to this emotional agility.

One more essential point of the empowered negotiation is the use of silence and pauses. Such methods can be used to help negotiators reassert an upper hand and incite the other side to contribute more information, and allow time to think seriously. Silence is a very useful resource in eliciting concessions and leading to more equitable discussion.

The empowered negotiators are also skilled at utilising available unique strengths and resources; regardless of whether it is their knowledge, contacts, or timing, they know how to leverage them in their favor. By concentrating on ethical leverage instead of taking force, they make the negotiation process proper and respectful.

The bottom line with empowered negotiation is about something bigger than closing deals. It is a project of creating lasting relations, establishing innovativeness, and achieving growth. Seeing a negotiation process as a journey and not a war enables individuals to explore new avenues and meet the goal of satisfying both sides of the dispute. Not only does this holistic approach improve the outputs of agreements, but it also leads to personal and professional growth, so every negotiation is one in the path of personal empowerment and overall success.

Chapter 2: Mindset Shifts for Negotiation Success

Debunking the Born Negotiator Myth

Some of the most prevalent misconceptions about the issue of the ability to negotiate include the assumption that one can either negotiate or not; this is an inborn trait that is not subject to learning. Such a belief frequently causes people not to work on their negotiation skills, which contributes to losing the chance to advance and become successful in many areas of life. However, negotiation is not an art that only a few have been gifted with, but a skill that anyone can develop and improve on the basis of practice and knowledge.

The issue of negotiation is viewed as an elusive art that only some individuals have. Popular culture and movies often portray the negotiator as a charismatic figure who can easily convince somebody to think the way he/she does. However, when skill acquisition is studied, it turns out that negotiation is not a gift of nature but a practice and several techniques that can be learned and perfected by everyone. Part of this learning process encompasses knowing and employing a set of micro-skills that includes preparation, active listening, framing, questioning, and emotional regulation.

Think about the experiences of a well-known negotiator who originally did not have the natural tendency toward negotiation. At an early stage in their career, they found it hard to command and confront others; they felt unequal in serious negotiations. With hard work and determination, they evolved into people who are negotiation pros. They have become a success case to support the notion that not everyone was born to be good at negotiations, but can achieve the same.

The meat of successful negotiation is the fundamental skills. Preparation is vital since it prepares the negotiators to be more aware of the environment, to expect obstacles, and to set concrete goals. Effective listening is also crucial because participants of the negotiation process can become aware of the needs of their counterparts and adapt their tactics to those needs. Framing and questioning serve to guide the conversation to a positive future where both sides win. In contrast, emotional control helps negotiators stay calm under pressure and not be distracted.

However, a lot of myths about the process of negotiation stop people. Projections, including, I am not tough enough, I hate conflict, or I am not a salesperson are obstacles that hold individuals back when it is time to negotiate. Nevertheless, these are myths that can be debunked by becoming educated and practicing. Negotiation does not demand inborn assertiveness; it can be entered into a calm and strategic state of mind.

Negotiation skills cannot be developed without a growth mindset. By adopting the concept that through determination and effort, people can develop their abilities, one can break the barriers of not venturing. Such an attitude inspires ongoing learning and practice, which is required to become proficient in the art of negotiation. It is also proposed that individuals be asked to look back at learning curves in other activities, such as fitness, coding, or leadership, to understand that negotiation is just a different area in which they can improve as well.

To fill the gap between theory and practice, the readers are advised to find a negotiation situation they have already experienced, even though it was of a small size or not conscious. This reflection can be used to identify and acknowledge the negotiation skills that they already have, and form the basis of improving those. By setting themselves up with the task of trying to get better at this, they are able to move their anxiety and self-doubt to confidence and ability. In this way, they can turn negotiation into an easy task rather than an arduous one.

Transforming Anxiety into Advantage

Anxiety is usually thought of as the enemy standing in the way of negotiations, but it can actually provide additional energy. A change of viewpoints starts with how adrenaline released into the body by anxiety has a physiological impact. Rather than consider this a weakness, this can be considered as a kind of eustress - the positive stress that makes it easier to stay focused and come up with creative ideas. It is important to reimagine anxiety to turn it into a negotiation strength.

Look at the science behind such a transformation. Anxiety causes the release of adrenaline, a reaction that prepares an individual to take action. Adequately harnessed, this improved level of alertness may be used to become better performers when under pressure. The trick is to harness this energy positively, harness it, and use it as an impetus to preparation and action, rather than to fly off the handle into a panicked state.

Some nervous energy can be productively directed with the help of practical exercises. Consider an example where a pre-negotiation ritual will create the atmosphere of success. This can be a checklist to help cover all the bases, deep breathing that relaxes one, and power poses that help one feel confident. The negotiator can feel grounded through such rituals and use the anxiety as a source of energy that helps the negotiator achieve success.

The other strong option is to come up with a confidence script. This is a list of promises or affirmations that a negotiator can repeat prior to getting engaged in a high-stakes discussion. It acts as a mental practice, firming up one's focus and instilling a positive mind frame. Such a script may be customized to ensure that the negotiator goes to the room with the foresight of what she is dealing with and with a goal in mind.

Situations that happen in reality are usually unpredictable and may activate anxiety. It is vital to know how to enter such moments. As an example, should one negotiator become tongue-tied in the middle of negotiations, being able to revive their tactical abilities is highly desirable. Anxiety can be avoided by avoiding rushing into things or being stuck in a situation where one has to say something or pose a question when no ideas come to mind. One can use techniques like pausing to think, asking clarification questions to buy time, or using scripts to steer the conversation back on track.

Self-compassion is a major factor in controlling anxiety. Preparing yourself to feel nervous and even deriving comfort from the idea that being nervous is a part of the process can be done simply by accepting that it is part of it and focusing on it with positivity. After every negotiation, looking back at what happened, acknowledging that even small wins are wins, and immediately applying new skills and lessons are all ways to develop and build resilience. Small victories can be used to boost confidence in the negotiator, with time bringing about a change in nervousness into a useful partner.

Finally, in order to verify professional negotiators, it is important to change the attitude toward anxiety and see it as an advantage rather than a liability. These strategies help people overcome the challenge that has once been regarded as a barrier and become effective negotiators, obtaining superior results. Besides the current gain, the transformation supports long-term personal and professional growth that allows achieving successes in the future.

Win-Win Mindset

In the sphere of negotiation, the ideology that a person applies to negotiations can significantly change the results. A win-win mindset represents a radical way of being that attempts to transcend the thinking process of the zero-sum game, where the gain of one is viewed as the loss of another. Rather, it adheres to the ideology that when cooperation and understanding exist between the two groups, both may end up being winners, whereby each gets to attain their most important goals.

The thinking characterising this mindset is a shift in thinking that is competitive to collective thinking. It forces negotiators to look at the negotiation table as a platform to solve problems rather than as a battleground. Through mutual gain orientation as opposed to individual win-win orientation, parties are persuaded to seek solutions that increase the pie as opposed to cutting it into small pieces. This would be an atmosphere and environment in which the innovative solutions would be more likely to become apparent as the interests of all involved are understood and incorporated.

The actual practice of a win-win attitude begins with a thorough knowledge of the other partner's needs and interests. This entails listening actively and the desire of the person to recognize the situation differently. By searching and finding the underlying wants and limits of each of the parties, the parties are able to develop proposals that satisfy the wants and limits of the parties, thereby creating value for all involved.

To be able to apply a win-win ideology, one needs to overcome the fear of being considered weak or too accommodating. Some negotiators are afraid to pursue mutual gain, as it may make them appear as pushovers. A win-win mindset does not, however, mean the sacrifice of the goals of another. Rather, it promotes aggressive communication and ethical negotiation approaches that fail to dismiss one's interests and yet remain open to the prospect of cooperation.

To develop this disposition, negotiators should ensure that they conduct due preparations prior to negotiations. This preparation includes getting knowledge of not only their personal targets and limitations, but also getting to know the background, needs, and possible limits of the other party. Going to the negotiation table prepared with facts, negotiators are in a better position to identify areas likely to give rise to synergy and formulate proposals that are appealing and achievable.

Also, strategic questioning may reveal the obscure interests and chances of cooperation. Questions that dig deeper into the priorities of the other party will divulge where mutual benefits can be achieved. This practice is helpful not only in terms of finding common ground but also in showing the sincerity of getting a mutually beneficial result, and this can foster a buildup of trust and rapport.

In reality, a win-win mentality can result in long-term deals and improved relations. By implementing a mindset that would emphasize the creation of value rather than only claiming value, negotiators have a chance of building partnerships that are flexible and adaptable to future changes. This will not only help both parties immediately regarding the negotiation, but will also enhance further work and trust.

To understand how a win-win attitude secures a successful finalization of negotiations, there must be a paradigm shift. It provokes negotiators to break free of the old adversarial ways and adopt a new spirit of cooperation. In such a way, they will open up new horizons of value creation, enable closer relationships, and provide positive outcomes to parties involved. Not only does such an attitude help individual negotiations, but it also benefits the overall collaborative working environment.

Overcoming Fear of Conflict

In the world of negotiation, fear of conflict is a terrible impasse, and it can be based on the discomfort that many have when they face the possibility of disagreement or confrontation. However, this fear is typical of any negotiator, even for experienced negotiators, and overcoming this fear is a vital key to successful negotiation.

Realizing that most humans experience the fear of conflict can be the beginning of overcoming it. Most successful professionals have had to conquer this fear in order to perform well at their workplaces, but basic strategies can help one learn more to deal with it. It should be understood that fear is part and parcel of us and not a show of weakness, as it can be a strength when tamed.

A useful strategy that one can use to deal with the unpleasant part of tough conversations is to do what is sometimes called disagree and commit. This approach will help participants to disagree appropriately and be committed to the decision arrived at by the group when it is made. It aids in the enhancement of a winnable ambiance regardless of a divided opinion.

Furthermore, the utilization of non-confrontational language and statements may help to resolve the escalation. By phrasing in terms that do not instill a sense of blame in others, negotiators can evade the power of defensiveness in others by stating their thoughts in a less accusatory manner. As an example, pointing out that "I believe this strategy may not be able to achieve our targets" rather than saying "you are wrong on this strategy" can go a long way in how your words will be accepted.

Role-playing may also be a great method of preparing to face a conflict. One can train to withstand situations when a person has to resist some unreasonable requests by simulating them and learning how to remain calm and represent themselves in the best light. This practice is an effective way to develop confidence and preparation to face negotiations in the real world.

Another very important factor in resolving the fear of conflict is the management of rejection and setbacks through resilience. It entails perceiving setbacks not as failures but as a way of expanding and educating. A useful tool would be to have a bounce-back reflection worksheet that would help people to think logically as to what went wrong in a negotiation and what the lesson of life that can be learnt.

It can be empowering as well to ask for feedback on a "no" received. It makes one understand the other side of the story and may tell what can be done better. Additionally, it expresses a sense of desire toward personal and professional development that can be applied to further negotiations and make them effective.

Long-term skills, such as assertiveness and boundary-setting, require acquisition and have the potential to speed up an individual's career. Learning to say no when it is needed is an effective way of saving oneself, and at the same time, never ruining relationships. It requires the ability to find a proper balance between being assertive and being courteous, making sure that the needs of the self are addressed, and at the same time allows the needs of others to be respected.

It is not a matter of not being afraid because you can be afraid in negotiation, but the key issue is to manage the fear. Practicing these tips, one will be able to turn possible anxiety into the driving force of effective negotiations and develop an environment in which an honest conversation and mutual respect can contribute to better results. By so doing, not only do they develop the ability to negotiate effectively, but they also develop effective working relationships.

Chapter 3: Preparation as Power

Crafting a Negotiation Blueprint

During the complicated process of negotiation, practice is a silent hero that prepares the ground for success. The success of any meaningful negotiation process is achieved through the careful development of a blueprint and a strategic approach to each step of the process. This blueprint should not just contain the list of objectives but a wide picture of the objectives, priorities, probable challenges, and innovative means to address those challenges.

The initial way of developing this blueprint is to set out your goals. What are you hoping to come out of the negotiation? Clarity of purpose is crucial, no matter what it is: a better salary, a more favorable contract, or a new partnership. Such clarity will permit you to concentrate your effort and control the stream of the negotiation in your own desirable directions. After setting the objectives, it is important to prioritize them. Not every goal is equally important, and by being aware of the strategic importance of each, it is possible to make strategic tradeoffs and continue to achieve the most important aims.

A good negotiation plan would include envisaging possible obstacles and barriers. Put yourself in the position of the other party and think about his or her interests and reasons. What do they tend to spirit to? By anticipating such obstacles, you can draft the responses and counterarguments in such a way that keeps the negotiation flowing. A more fluid dialogue can be done because this anticipation eliminates most surprises and, rather, creates confidence.

Creativity is an essential part of the negotiation process, and you should have innovative solutions and alternatives in place in the blueprint. These are the instruments that can transform a deadlock into an opportunity. Suggestions such as having flexible terms, considerations for joining in joint ventures, or value-added services can broaden the opportunities and can be arrived at to mutual advantage.

Another very important element of the negotiation blueprint is documentation. Keep elaborate notes and records of how you are preparing, all research, strategy outlines, and possible scenarios. Not only does this documentation prove useful during preparation, but it is also a helpful reference tool during the negotiation itself, as nothing is missed or lost.

One of the tools in preparation for negotiation is visualization. Make a vision of the negotiation process, practicing how you think you are going to negotiate. These might assist you in maintaining a calm head in stressful conditions. Visualization helps to develop confidence, too, as you self-examine different situations and results.

The negotiation blueprint is an evolutionary fixture. It must also be dynamic and versatile so that it can develop as the negotiation goes on. Learn to change your plan depending on new facts and circumstantial changes. A good negotiator knows how to move and adjust, following the blueprint as a guideline and not something that should be used step-by-step.

The making of the negotiation blueprint is, in the end, a process of empowerment through knowledge and strategy. It is about preparing the scene that will make the negotiation successful by knowing, planning, and preparing innovative solutions to anticipated challenges. Having a thorough blueprint lets you go to the bargaining table confidently and clearly on which route the discussion should take to have a successful ending.

Understanding BATNA and ZOPA

The concepts of BATNA (Best Alternative to a Negotiated Agreement) and ZOPA (Zone of Possible Agreement) are the fundamental ones being used in the sphere of negotiations to comprehend and track the process of negotiations. BATNA is the best alternative plan of action that can be adopted by a party in the event of failure in the negotiation process, where both parties fail to come up with an agreement. It is basically the contingency measure that will prevent a negotiator from ending up with an undesirable solution. Understanding of your BATNA gives you a bottom limit, under which you do not have to accept an agreement, allowing the negotiators to make a choice calmly and without the fear of compromising.

To come up with a strong BATNA, one has to prepare well and analyse. It presupposes the discovery of all the available options, determining their feasibility, and the choice of the most promising one. The process also requires an analytical evaluation of possible scenarios and resources necessary to present them. In addition to having a safety net, BATNA can also provide a negotiator with confidence to negotiate on the basis of strength.

ZOOPA, as opposed to this, denotes the scope within which a deal can be acceptable to both sides of a negotiation. It is the intersection of the lowest one party is prepared to receive and the highest the other party is prepared to give. It is important to understand the ZOPA so as to determine the possibility of a successful negotiation. It demands a well-understood interest of both sides and their priorities and limitations.

The establishment of the ZOPA starts with a detailed examination of the needs and wants of the parties. This includes communicating openly and, in some cases, engaging in creativity when it comes to the problem-solving process so as to widen the realm of solutions that may satisfy both sides of the relationship. The ZOPA might not be that obvious; sometimes, it may be needed to scratch the surface-level positions to reveal the sets of interests that can be used to establish mutually beneficial agreements.

BATNA and ZOPA are factors that contribute to negotiations since they are dynamic and strategic. Whereas BATNA establishes the maximum range to which an acceptable outcome can be subjected, ZOPA provides the range through which the points of outcome negotiation can occur. A negotiator with final alternatives in a high state can extend the ZOPA towards his/her parameters. On the other hand, a negotiator with an unclear BATNA can be caught in a tiny ZOPA and lack bargaining power as well as attractive terms.

A good negotiator uses the insight they gained when processing BATNA and ZOPA to develop tactics that can offer the best deal as well as create a constructive mood. This is not only limited to the own BATNA and ZOPA but also the estimate of the other party. In so doing, negotiators will awaken to the bottom line of the other side and are thus enabled to prepare themselves to adjust their strategy.

Theory In reality, competent use of BATNA and ZOPA can turn negotiation into a partnership-based problem-solving problem rather than a stand-off between the protagonists. Negotiators who successfully maneuver through these notions are better placed to get outcomes that are not just satisfying but also sustainable and that can set the stage for lasting partnerships and future success.

Digital Research Hacks

In the modern fast-paced digital environment, research ability has been a very important skill to possess, particularly in the preparation for negotiations. With appropriate digitalization, it is possible to discover useful information about the negotiating partners and thus have the potential to make more calculated decisions. Having a plethora of platforms to use, one needs to find ways to integrate them and use them to develop comprehensive approaches in their negotiations.

LinkedIn is unique because such a degree of information exists about professional experiences, relationships, and organizations, and it is available to individuals. One can learn more about the professional history of a counterpart and people who may influence them due to the knowledge of the mutual connections and the work history. Similarly, databases such as Crunchbase offer information on the financial well-being of a firm, recent financing rounds, participating investors, and strategic direction, which can be invaluable in developing a deeper understanding of the larger environment that a given firm competes in.

Press releases and Google News are essential when keeping up to date with the latest news that could impact the negotiation environment. These sources are able to shed more light on changes in company strategy, announcements made in public, or changes in the market that might affect the negotiation process. Staying abreast of these changes, negotiators are able to anticipate better the goings-on and the thought processes of their counterparts.

Although digital research can provide very strong insights, care should be taken in order to avoid entering into grey areas that may be of ethical concern. To a point, digging too deep and being too prepared can be intrusive, and it can hurt the relationship as well as the negotiations. Between complete research and privacy, it is important to bring correlated information that is well-derived and not a complete violation of assertions of privacy.

It is helpful to have a regulated framework for dealing with digital research to ease it through these nuances. The development of a digital research checklist would help simplify the process and help avoid both under- and over-reaching. Such a checklist may involve checking up-to-date company news, revisiting professional profiles, and noticing any mutual acquaintances or common interests that may be used to help build rapport.

In addition, it is in the synthesis and development of actionable strategies that the real strength of digital research presents itself. By determining the pressures, objectives, and negotiation style of the other party, one can create a counter strategy that will either comply with or fight back against them. This could entail adapting to the bargaining position according to what the counterpart seems to consider most important, or even pronouncing the objections indicated according to the obstacles that the company has faced recently.

In a nutshell, digital research is not about data collection but about translating data and turning it into strategic implications that enable decision makers to make informed decisions during negotiation. Using the right tools and sticking to ethical practices, the negotiators can prepare better, predict possible issues, and bargain in a state of confidence and clarity. Such a proactive stance not only increases the probability of getting desirable results. Still, it serves to reinforce professional relations as it shows their dedication and regard towards the negotiating process.

Setting Non-Negotiables

It is always important to have on paper what you are non-negotiable about before plunging into any negotiations. This phase places the skeleton of your negotiation strategy, and that is not to lose track of your cardinal values and priorities in the given negotiation. Determining these non-negotiables takes soul searching and a sound idea of what you can accept and what will be unacceptable to you. This directness is essential in that it does not allow the negotiating situation or the persuasive skills of the other side to pull you into its charms.

To start with, think of the conditions that will make a deal unacceptable despite the possible advantages. These non-negotiables need to be formulated and written down as a reminder when it comes to negotiations. It can help to construct a worksheet in which you define these essential issues, as well as those issues on which you have compromises. As an example, during the job negotiation process, non-negotiables can be the salary and benefits, whereas such aspects as job title can be more precise. The terms of payment may be non-negotiable in a business deal, but there may be leeway on the project scope.

When these parameters have been established, effective communication should be maintained. The words to be employed must be confident and cooperative, and must not establish an oppositional environment but maintain the boundaries in place. Such constructions as "This term is obligatory to us to go on with it" can also sound reasonably firm and non-aggressive.

Failure to set and communicate these non-negotiables can have unpleasant endings. There are warning stories of negotiations that failed because parties failed to clearly spell out their dealbreakers, resulting in eleventh-hour shocks and failure of talks. A mini case study can be presented to illustrate a situation where a negotiation has failed because of one party failing to present their red lines effectively, recommending the need to prepare the red lines before embarking on negotiations.

When confronted with the unforeseen, a list of non-negotiables would allow you to handle twists and turns with poise. Rehearsing possible scenarios and reactions to them would allow you to keep control of the negotiation in case it takes a direction that was not expected. This is a combination not only of being ready in the physical sense, like having a car, a place to stay, etc., but also being ready psychologically to leave and no longer accept continued mistreatment when your core needs are being ignored in order to define your boundaries.

At the end of the day, the setting of non-negotiables is all about empowering. It arms you with the skills to uphold honesty and focus so that every negotiation is carried out with regard to the strategic goals at hand. Not only will this defend your interest, but it will also commend respect in the eyes of the other party, who will see how clear and determined you are in your stances. By firmly grounding your negotiating approach to established non-negotiables, you establish a path to positive results, no matter how the process above may yield certain obstacles.

Chapter 4: Communication Micro-Skills

The Art of Anchoring

As far as the negotiation is concerned, anchoring has become one of the most critical concepts, which can yield a powerful impact on the process. Anchoring refers to the process of opening the negotiation with an offer or a position. This first bid, regardless of its mode of delivery and environment (e.g., face-to-face vs. digital), serves as a psychological anchor that can materialize the rest of the negotiation procedure.

The strength of the anchoring is the psychological effect it creates. A broad body of behavioral economics research notes that opening an offer in a negotiation can have a significant impact on the area of the potential agreement. This is because the first offer usually gives the grounds of expectation and forms a basis on which any future offer and counteroffer are compared. This means that the party may also apply an anchoring strategy to oneself, usually a strategic advantage, informally influencing the negotiation in a desirable direction.

Writing a strong anchor takes a level of confidence and critical thinking. It is not a simple act of throwing out a figure; it is an act of establishing an atmosphere and a pattern to work within during a negotiation. The trick is in defining the degree of aggressiveness or conservativeness the anchor should have, and this depends on the given situation of the negotiation. When anchored properly, this kind of anchor can be a highly effective tool to steer the discussion to acceptable terms and strike a balance between ambitiousness and plausibility.

In online negotiations, where conversations are conducted via email or via a video chat, anchoring is a trick that must be well thought through in terms of language and presentation. Not being physically present makes it hard to emphasize confidence and clarity, so it is quite necessary to use clear language and properly constructed arguments. The following phrases are suggested: given the scope and value, I suggest... Based on industry standards, one recommends.... Having said that, you can make a professional impression by using an anchor, thereby creating credibility.

Nonetheless, there are issues with anchoring. Once the other party throws its anchor in the negotiation, it is important to be in a position to adjust the negotiation. Responding calmly and tactically to a lowball or highball anchor and making a sufficient number of counteroffers can allow you to restore control of the narrative. It is about taking notice of the flag that has been planted, but then skilfully giving a counter-stroke to bring the conversation back to more favorable ground.

Another technique required in the art of anchoring is the subtlety of time and delivery. The introduction of an anchor at the wrong time may be interpreted as premature or squandered due to the cue that the proper time to exchange anchors would have passed. Thus, the placement alone is as important as the content of the anchor itself.

It is important to remember that to learn to anchor effectively, it is necessary to learn to understand human psychology. It is not just the initial offer being highly placed; it includes being ready to change and adjust to the moves of the negotiation. Using the power of anchoring, negotiating parties can shift discussions in their favor, towards the results desired based on their negotiating goals, and often create an atmosphere of mutual respect and cooperation.

Reading Digital Body Language

In the world of online communication, one of the key skills to use during the process of negotiations is digital body language. Previously, the cues that were used to facilitate in-person relations have evolved to a virtual world, with video conferencing and other text-based communication being the new standard. These new signals have to be understood to enable a gauge of engagement, resistance identification, and effective communication.

Video conferencing and facial expressions offer very important clues to the mental state of one of the participants. A furrowed brow may indicate confusion or disagreement, whereas a nod may indicate agreement or understanding.

However, physical presence is not there, which creates a chance of misinterpretation. A late answer in a chat may be misunderstood as a lack of interest, when again, this may be due to multitasking.

It is also important to develop self-awareness of what your digital body language is. Camera placement, maintaining eye contact with the other person, and gestures are some of the ways to improve clarity and warmth of virtual interaction. The use of these elements enables showing attention and seriousness, and minimizes the possibility of misunderstanding.

The tone of the written messages is another of the layers to take into account in the context of digital communication. Words, punctuation, and even emojis can severely change the tone. An example is a thumbs-up emoji, which means something different from an okay written word, depending on the context of its reading and the person to whom it is directed.

Misinterpretations are typical when using digital environments, and one should come up with mechanisms to overcome such difficulties. A guide that helps to troubleshoot can be of immense assistance when the sounds are confusing or when there is a conflict in the messages. By asking clarifying questions that are neither accusative nor open-ended, they help with breaking down the misunderstandings and do not increase tensions.

In virtual negotiations, part of reading digital body language would be to identify the exits, so you can recognize when someone is engaged or not. The timely responsiveness and the tone of written communication are key parts of this process. Being trained to make appropriate adjustments to personal online persona and learn how to project self-confidence and clarity can also make a significant difference in the results of the negotiations.

Further, it will help to be mindful of the pitfalls of digital communication. An example of such is silence, which can easily be misinterpreted. Silence in a physical gathering can be construed as thinking, but in the virtual world, it can be assumed that the party is bored. Likewise, text-based communications are disembodied, which can give rise to misunderstanding the intent or attitude of the other side.

The main way we can move through these complexities is to become proactive. This includes getting ready before the virtual meetup by having your technological side in place, making the environment accommodating enough, and listening to the cues of electronic body language. With increased practice, such skills may improve and minimize the chances of miscommunication and increase reading the room, even in virtual settings.

The bottom line is that the art of mastering the digital body language is learning to cope with the art of communicating. It involves a sensibility that pivots between tactical communication strategies and a sense of the digital environment. By mastering these skills, negotiators are able to read the digital room better, so their messages get interpreted the way they expect, and they correctly interpret the actions of others.

High-Precision Questions

Expertise in negotiation usually relies on the capacity to pose questions that dispel the clutter and expose why the other party is or is not behaving in a certain way. High-precision questions are weapons that, when used with skill and care, can turn a negotiation upside down as hidden motives are exposed. Such questions do not merely involve the acquisition of information but also efforts to provide insights that will transform the course of a dialogue.

First of all, high-precision questions are open in nature. Such questions are typically open-ended in nature, as opposed to yes-or-no questions, in that they encourage the other party to be more forthcoming than they were planning to be. This is the key component as it enables the negotiators to find out all features in a matter of possibilities and constraints. An example here is to say, What are your priorities in this deal? Cultivating this (probably through a more in-depth approach) may increase the level of knowledge as to what the other side most values, which may not be obvious from their high-level position.

In addition, they are distinguished by the specificity of high-precision questions. Such questions are designed to ask questions in specific areas of judgment or interest. They would guide the negotiators in identifying the gripping point that may be guiding the other party in coming up with decisions. A query such as the following: - Can you take me through your decision-making process? First, it does not simply demand answers. Still, it encourages the respondent to come forth with information pertaining to any external stress or internal parameters that may be distorting their decisions.

High-precision questioning is characterised by the strategy of asking questions in sequence. Beginning with general questions and then progressively zooming in to more specific ones, a negotiator can direct the discussion to a higher level of insight. This process gives a step-by-step realization of the situation as one responds to the other, in turn revealing the details of the other's position. For example, a negotiator may ask the following question: What are your primary objectives? Later on, ask how it affects your flexibility in the time frame for these goals. This sequence will help reveal priorities as well as help to chart out possible points of give and take.

There is also a higher-stakes task to use high-precision questions to uncover latent objections or snagging issues that may not be evident. By inquiry, is there something that would bar us from going ahead? With the negotiators, the identification and resolution of whatever concerns the negotiators may have as a stumbling block can be done in advance. These questions not only show the possible problems but also show the willingness to cooperate in order to seek solutions.

Besides uncovering lurking motives and objections, high-precision queries can be used to spot key people who may not be at the negotiation table but who influence the process. An example is inquiries such as, "Do we have any internal stakeholders we haven't considered yet?" This practice makes the other listen to more than the present conversation, but also consider the wider factors that affected the situation.

The ability to use high-precision questions is a combination of curiosity and strategy. The negotiators need to be keen listeners, i.e., able to adjust the direction of their questioning according to the answers that they get. This versatility makes the conversation dynamic and moving with the change of the territory where the negotiation is taking place.

To recap, questions of high precision should be an important asset of the negotiator that can open up more facets and result in a more open and cooperative conversation. With these emphases on open-ended, specific, strategically sequenced inquiry, negotiators should find that the process of the negotiation can become a more fully-informed and adequately successful joint inquisition, ultimately resulting in negotiated outcomes that are better aligned with the actual interests and needs of all the parties to the negotiation.

Active Listening

As a dance of negotiations becomes more complex, the art of listening steps into the limelight, which creates the tapestry of insights between them. Listening during a negotiation is critical to success as one goes through the high-stress space by ensuring that originally adversarial situations turn into a collaborative one. As the practice of listening actively helps to uncover even more information, it can aid in the de-escalation of hostilities and create an environment of trust and tolerance between the parties.

Active listening is centered on the concept of reflective paraphrasing. This is responding to what the other party has said and not just as an echo, but as an expedient in demonstrating that you have listened and understood their message. The technique fulfills two functions: it can confirm to the speaker that he or she has been heard, and it can help a listener confirm his or her understanding, minimizing the chance of misunderstandings. Summarizing and validating emotional signals also helps boost this process in that it recognizes the feelings and apprehensions of the speaker, which are, in many cases, just as important as the facts being reported.

In anticipation of negotiation, quick, live listening training may go a long way in getting one battle-ready. The partner work may be used in an exercise of repeating and rephrasing. Couple up, and take turns rephrasing the younger person. During a five-minute session, the participants are asked to act in turns, saying a point, following which the other notes down his/her own understanding of what was said. The exercise helps to hone the skill of listening to essential patterns and themes in the other party's statements, which is an important skill when in a negotiation.

Inactive listening, or silence, is not generally assessed. Moments of silence create space in which the other party can say more and add more layers of thought to the information. Small encouragers, including nodding one's head and verbally saying something brief like, "I am listening," or "Tell me more of that," express that one is listening and thereby encourage the speaker to continue talking.

Active listening needs tactical application beyond information gathering; it is an effective method of defusing an aggressive situation. During the escalation of tensions, paraphrasing may convert the strain into a constructive conversation. One can change the attitude of the listener, e.g., by presenting a controversial phrase in the form of a question, or a suggestion to be discussed, in order to make the listener look at the case as a collaboration, rather than a battle. These techniques not only de-escalate tension but also create a ground of trust because they show an ability to entertain and show respect to the other side of the case.

It also takes the form of preparing oneself with scripted lines when one feels that they might want to confront another or have an emotional blow-up. Constructs such as: "Let me stop and take a moment to make sure we are on the same page" or "That is a good point, and I need to think about that" can get time and eliminate pressure to respond to regain composure and get back on track. The use of the so-called acknowledge and pivot method, when the feeling or dissent is addressed and only then a shift in the discourse towards the problems presented is made, is especially useful in ensuring that the discussion is productive.

Overall, active listening involves more than hearing words; it is the process of moving to a deeper form of communication that takes into consideration both what is said and what is not said. By learning to work with this skill, negotiation experts can strengthen their skills in maneuvering through much more complicated negotiations, which means that the negotiators and their counterparties will be able to find common ground and succeed in their negotiations.

Chapter 5: Ethical Leverage and Influence

Building Ethical Leverage

A leverage is a key concept in any negotiation. However, the road to the creation of leverage (ethically) is subject to misinterpretation. The process starts with a redefinition of leverage not as a force of pressure but as a source of mutual-value creation. The true leverage involves a breakthrough knowledge of the needs and limitations of both parties and the ability to develop solutions that represent a win for both parties.

Transparency and trust form the base of ethics leverage. It demands a subtle form of strategic thinking where, instead of smashing the party, you are trying to engage in an information exchange with the goal of creating an atmosphere in which both parties feel free to exchange information without intimidation. This openness may give way to unexpected revelations that open the way to inspirational solutions.

One of the best strategies to develop ethical leverage is to enlarge the set of possible consequences. As an alternative to the fixed pie theory of negotiation, think of multiplier effects by finding issues in which you and the other party are mutually interested. This could include bundling services, investigating flexible payments, and finding cost-reducing alternatives that will not compromise value. The next way to structure the negotiation is to expand it. By widening the range of subjects in negotiations, each party can uncover points of agreement that may not have been obvious at the beginning.

Moreover, there is ethical leverage, which comprises timing and alternative mastery. Knowing when to offer a price, when to withdraw, and when to walk out are essential elements. This is not to be used as a method of manipulation but as a natural understanding of the dynamics of a negotiating process. Likewise, developing alternatives- called BATNA (Best Alternative to a Negotiated Agreement)- provides a back-up cushion that can give negotiators the comfort of not having to become belligerent in the deal and have their way on one or more issues.

Influence and manipulation tend to be mixed up in the face of negotiation. The tenet of ethical leverage means that leverage rests on influence, which is premised on the idea of persuasion and mutual gain, as opposed to manipulation, which is aimed at control or deceit. Negotiators are expected to persuade people and make the best rational appeal backed up by facts and reason instead of using force and deception.

Such tools as the use of "if/then" statements can be beneficial to ensuring ethics. These statements make it clear under what circumstances the agreements can be made so that both sides know what it is about and the consequences of the agreement. Examples could include, "Meet this deadline and we can talk about a bigger order," which creates clear expectation levels and not a confrontational environment.

Ethical dilemmas frequently occur when the negotiation process is tempted to manipulate the market with the use of dirty tricks. The ethical decision also pays dividends because, in addition to keeping clean, you gain the advantage of relationships that can be more effective than an individual transaction. Negotiators must take into account the long-term outcome of their decisions rather than the immediate benefits if such a dilemma confronts them, and they should place ethical norms above any other profit.

In short, it is not all the elements of building ethical leverage. It is about developing a negotiation setting in which trust, transparency, and mutual reward are prioritized. By dwelling on these tenets, can negotiators forge lasting partnerships and get good results that are not only positive but also sustainable?

Personalizing Your Style

Knowing how he/she negotiates is a key element in the process of being a good communicator. All people are unique and have their own strengths and preferences when entering the negotiating table, formed by their personality and experiences. Understanding such characteristics and using them to advantage will certainly increase the success one may have in a keyword.

There are three broad classifications of individuals on the basis of their personality traits: introverts, extroverts, and ambiverts. All the types possess their strengths that can be used during negotiations. Introverts, for example, are proactive in listening and preparation. They have the capacity to think and to be detail-oriented, thereby enabling them to foresee the path and to establish strategic measures. During negotiation, introverts can use their listening skills well to ensure that they understand the needs of the other party and, thus, are essential to developing win-win situations.

On the one hand, extroverts usually enjoy social life and are good at establishing rapport and relationships. They can use their natural charisma and ease of relating to other people to their advantage, as trust and enthusiasm are paramount in a negotiation. Extroverts can use their social skills to establish an atmosphere of openness and optimism and hence promote more collaborative discussions.

Ambiverts are endowed with the qualities of both introverts and extroverts, and they can hence change their style to suit their situations. This can prove very useful where one needs a balance between the ability to listen and to be assertive during negotiations. Ambiverts are also capable of dampening their style to adjust to the negotiation dynamics and thus handle a variety of scenarios and people.

Being aware of one's negotiation style is not enough. It is also important to come up with strategies that supplement such natural inclinations. Introverts, in this case, may prefer to take time to prepare well before a negotiation and resort to the use of written messages more effectively in order to express their ideas clearly. They can also learn to practice active listening skills to make sure they pick up all verbal and non-verbal cues in discussions.

Extroverts, on the other hand, could work on developing their listening skills and ensuring they do not talk much. By curbing their instincts and becoming attentive, they will be able to assure themselves that they are not defending their desires to serve their interests only.

After the ambivert, the conflict is managing when to apply his/her tendencies towards extroversion or introversion. This flexibility can be trained by practicing mindfulness and introspection so that they can seamlessly accommodate a change of gears in the negotiation process.

More than personal styles, effective negotiation also requires becoming knowledgeable about the style adopted by the counterpart, so as to make adjustments. This takes a high degree of observation and understanding, because it is important to read the cues and desires of the other party so as to structure offers and counteroffers in such a way as to minimize losses.

The ideal state of affairs is to tailor the manner of negotiating to personal qualities and still be willing to learn and evolve. It is an act of self-awareness and sustained learning that one should engage in to make sure that their approach in a negotiation would improve with each round of the action. In acting that way, negotiators have become more effective and more collaborative when it comes to their professional and personal relationships.

The Power of Silence

Silence does not appear as a vacuum in the world of negotiation; rather, it is an effective tool that creates its presence. One does not necessarily have to speak to change the dynamics of a conversation, as silence can change the direction of the conversation and bring in a new emphasis. This nonspatial, but powerful aspect of communications is worthy of being a negotiation tool because it can be used strategically to sway or persuade.

The effect of silence is psychological and engraved in the hearts of human beings. Having a feeling of discomfort with silence drives people to fill the silence with talk. Such unease can be utilized to the benefit during negotiations. Successful use of the strategic pause allows negotiators to take back command of the negotiation, inducing concessions or causing a negotiator to reveal more information than s/he might have intended. The method entails deliberately leaving a silence after presenting an offer or reacting to a turn of phrase that a person did not expect, thus leaving the space open that forces the interlocutor to fill it, directly exposing him/her and his/her mind.

Silence, too, is a great way to make tensions dissolve. When it comes to high-stakes negotiation, passions get hot, and words can make things worse. By omitting talk, a negotiator gives time to the emotions to calm down and gives every party time to re-adjust what they are going to respond. This hesitation has the potential to stop it in its tracks and allow them to think with a more logical and creative temperament of problem-solving.

Nevertheless, silence is a strategic tool that has to be carefully employed and adequately administered. Abused or used in the wrong context, overuse may cause failure to engage, particularly in digital or virtual situations where the visual clue to participation may be missing and the silence may be misinterpreted as a lack of interest or attention. Thus, it is imperative to learn how to read the room when one is feeling the brunt of silence in terms of truly facilitating discomfort so as to break out of a communication block rather than indicating a communication stumble.

Merged with active listening, the power of silence is even strengthened. By staying silent, negotiators can pay complete attention to the words of their communication partner and notice details and emotional differences that could not be detected in the case of speaking. Such keen listening goes beyond creating a rapport and also gives invaluable information about the priorities and the concerns of the other party.

In addition, silence may serve as a mirror, responding to the other party with his/her words. It is able to induce self-examination, making them change their stances or tone. Such a reflective nature of silence may provide a solution to stalled negotiations, making way for compromise and collaboration.

In essence, the magic of silence is situated in its two-fold nature, namely, the leverage and the creativity. By learning where and when to use silence, negotiators can improve their skills at navigating tricky situations where they can make sure thoughtful conversation and mutual understanding are present. Therefore, silence is not just quietness; it is a tactical gap that can even turn the course of the negotiation table towards the side that brings it to play with prudence.

Identifying Hidden Agendas

In the multifaceted world of negotiation, a hidden agenda is one of the most important aspects to understand and identify in order to meet the desired end of the quest. Hidden agendas are the non-verbal goals or motives that people or parties introduce into the situation, and normally under the cover of the overt goals they articulate. These agendas may be either personal, organizational, or political in nature, and they are usually an ingredient in most negotiation interactions.

This will make it very difficult to identify these hidden motives since it will take a keen sense of observation and a strategic approach. A good way to do this is by using probing techniques and indirect questioning. By posing general questions such as, "What do you think success is to you?" Questions such as "Are internal priorities that I need to know about?" help negotiators to unearth underlying interests that at that moment may not be visible. Not only does this technique unmask ulterior motives, but it is also used to better understand the needs of the other party and their limitations.

Some red flags that may be an indication of a not-so-obvious agenda would be the use of contradictory statements, not wanting to share information, or abrupt changes in demands. As an example, a stakeholder entering the negotiation process late with some new demands may signal some hidden priorities. The ability to identify these signs early can help negotiators calibrate their strategy in time, so that they do not get surprised by these events unfolding.

It can be difficult to negotiate when there is a lack of clarity in the agenda of each party. Yet, it may be possible to open up a conversation that will help to identify common areas of interest and seek transparency. Proper communication, where a free dialogue is encouraged, together with a clear understanding of expectations, can result in constructive and helpful talks. Also, it is important to formulate contingency plans in situations where there is a possibility of some people having concealed interests that can disrupt the negotiation process. It is by anticipating the upset that negotiators can remain in control and be able to navigate the dialogue back to areas of win-win.

Adding behavioral economics concepts can also be used to increase the exposure of hidden agendas and to manage them. Recognizing cognitive biases like the anchoring effect or loss aversion can add to our knowledge on how the parties are going to prioritize some types of outcomes over others. Needing to have such biases in mind, negotiators can construct a context where latent interests come out and are dealt with in a formative manner.

The point is that there is essentially an individual hazard in dealing with those who have hidden plans that are more conducive to a climate of negotiation where honesty and group work are respected. This means establishing the environment in which every one of the parties feels free to communicate genuine wants and concerns without the apprehension of being judged. By so doing, negotiators can turn potential tensions into paths of the partnership and innovation, opening the door to solutions that would meet both overt and convergent goals.

Overall, detecting some ulterior intentions demands a set of effective strategic questions, being able to look and see, and being ready to participate in full dialogue. By catching the cues of concealed interests and applying methods of bringing them to light, negotiators will feel free to discourse with one another without ambiguity and with greater success and sustainability.

Chapter 6: Navigating Difficult Negotiations

Cross-Cultural Cues

Cross-cultural signals are an important aspect in the world of negotiations, where such issues may be critical to the process of making a deal. Subtleties of cultural disparity can be present in many forms; they determine negotiations, anticipations, and approaches. The significant feature is the direct and indirect ways of communication. Whereas some cultures find it important to be very clear and direct, some other cultures may appreciate a less pronounced method, where the messages are soft and implied. The difference between the two is vital in the light of the negotiators since it determines how they offer proposals and how they take them.

The other major aspect is the attitude to hierarchy. Some cultures have a strongly innate hierarchical set-up, and respect towards authority figures is of the utmost value. This can affect the conduct of negotiations, e.g., who speaks and how to make decisions. In more egalitarian cultures, on the other hand, the negotiations may be more collegial with the participation of all parties ranking encouraged.

There are also cultural differences in time perception that apply to the negotiation speed and structure. Particular cultures perceive time as a linear utilitarian material with a specific focus on the use of time, such as punctuality and deadlines. In contrast, other cultures consider time to be a fluid item, a flexible time. When not handled properly, this may create misunderstanding with either party perceiving the other as either unwilling or in a hurry.

In order to overcome these cultural differences, a lot of pre-negotiation research is required. This would be in the form of knowing about the holidays, taboos, and the most appropriate way to address the culture of the negotiating party. This sort of preparation prevents unintentional offense and encourages a respectful dialogue. Examples of such suggestions include the use of formal titles or the effort to avoid slang in a way that expresses deference and the awareness of cultural expectations.

In addition, cultural sensitivity is stressed by illustrating practical examples in the real world. There have been cases where transactions almost collapsed because of a gestured signal or phrase that was misinterpreted. These warning stories are used as reminders of the problems involved in cross-cultural negotiations and being careful of these subtleties.

Besides the preparation, flexibility in the negotiation process is crucial. The establishment of a connection with other people may be achieved by using cultural rules as guidelines for defining language and behavior, which helps avoid misunderstanding and establishes rapport. As another example, indirect communication is a more useful approach in cultures where the value of such behavior is high.

Lastly, it is vital to recognize that there may be a risk of cultural miscommunication and to be receptive to answers and make it known that one wants to learn. Asking counterparts to highlight any ambiguous or inappropriate wording instills the trust of mutual respect and understanding. These tactics not only improve the process of negotiation but also help to create longer-term, cross-cultural relationships.

Handling Deadlocks

Digital negotiations have a lot of deadlocks. Such impasses tend to ensue when communication gets blocked, where email chains come to a dead end or video-conference calls end in unwillingness to reach a consensus. It is important to identify the indicators of a deadlock early enough since they can provide the negotiators with the chance to use the strategies to eliminate the deadlock before it cannot be overcome.

Principled negotiation is one of the effective ways of getting out of a deadlock. This approach is concerned with interests and not positions, which would enable the parties to locate deeper motivations and needs other than finding themselves trapped with particular demands. A re-framing of issues can help negotiators find creative solutions that would have been otherwise unidentified because they shifted the underlying discussion to that which is of real value to the parties.

The other strong tool is the creation of creative options. Having the parties brainstorm with no immediate evaluation will allow for finding solutions that do not counter the interests of all parties. This inter-vener or inter-disciplinary method can shift an antagonistic stalemate into a mutual problem-solving event, a form of comradeship feeling and intent.

What is next in case of a non-X: Y? The technique is a certain trick in this framework that opens up new grounds for the discussion. By suggesting alternative scenarios, negotiators can deflect the rigid positions of discussion and move towards mutually rewarding and flexible outcomes. This is not only a progress-inducing technique, but it also shows readiness to compromise and meet halfway.

It is acceptable in some instances where direct negotiation is deemed insufficient that third-party facilitators or mediators are brought on board. These outside experts are able to present new opinions and bring the discussions back on track. Their existence may also help to neutralize power relations to guarantee that every voice will be heard and taken into account.

Whenever the negotiation is at a high-tension level, it can be a good strategy to request a pause and to restart the process. By taking a break, emotional feelings are allowed to calm down, and parties have time to consider their own side of the family negotiation as well as the situation as a whole.

This break can be constructive in that parties will be able to reconvene with a sharper focus and a clearer mindset.

The initiative of citing a cooling-off period can also be discussed as a tactical action other than a trade-off. By offering it as a joint chance of reflection and re-grouping, negotiators are able to hold their ground without having to appear to give in. This strategy highlights the need to be professional and allow a level head, despite the hard negotiating.

In virtual settings, the possibility of a stand-off is amplified because of the loss of physical presence in the situation and the risks of miscommunication. Accordingly, in order to make the most of the strategies offered, it is highly important to be able to keep an eye on the challenges of digital negotiations, including tone adjustment and the wise employment of written means of communication. The use of these approaches wisely means that negotiators will be able to overcome impasse situations skillfully so as to end up with outcomes that are satisfactory and fair to all parties.

Multi-Party Scenarios

Multi-party situations create another dimension to the art of negotiation that demands skilled tactfulness and balancing in the mixing of different parties. Such situations, frequently known as gang-up situations, require the negotiators to manage the development of multiple interests and personalities deftly. The central case of such interactions is the need to determine the power structure and the risks that may arise while negotiating with multiple counterparts at once.

The potential of groupthink, triangulation, and alliance-building behavior is one of the strongest elements in appropriately managing the scenarios. Groupthink may tend to bring forth a similarity in ideas that does not necessarily favour all the involved parties. This means that negotiators need to be wary of such tendencies so individual views do not become diluted by the groupthink. Triangulation is also a potential issue with one party trying to play off against another party by seeking to split and conquer. Likewise, building alliances can tip the power balance, and thus a good understanding of the underlying alliances and their behaviour during the negotiation process becomes essential.

Multi-party meetings are meetings that require careful laying out of known coalitions and emerging coalitions. The appointment of a specific agenda and duties beforehand may aid in showing order and concentration in the discussions. Such preparation would enable the negotiators to control and manipulate the direction of the conversation and to ensure that everyone is given a chance to be heard and to negotiate without one party taking center stage. When one feels outnumbered or out of control, having pre-scripted responses that one can use is always helpful. Easy statements like, "I would like to take a break so that I can respond to each of the points you presented," or, "Do you think we could go around the group to give everyone a chance to speak?" It can assist in balancing and making the conversation on the right path.

The important strategic value of building coalitions and finding allies within the group can be used to help improve bargaining power. By advocating mutual interests and gaining the assistance of potential supporters privately before the meeting, negotiators can build a network of supporters that will come in handy during the negotiations. This would not only give a stronger position but would also help in building a team-oriented environment where there are shared interests and not over personal gains.

In those cases when the negotiations break down or have become confrontational, then it may be required that the talks go to a higher level. It is important to see the signs of a deadlock, like having constant disputes or the authorities reaching their limits. It is an art to change the situation raised by escalation without insulting parties and damaging relationships. As an example, saying something like, "To make sure we nail this, I would appreciate the input of my manager/legal team" will allow bringing the manager or legal team on board in a way that is respectful and professional to both parties.

All in all, the idealized outcome of multi-party negotiations is to create value and long-term relationships. Concentrating on pie enlargement and winning-win solutions, the negotiators will be in a position to create an aura of success and win-win situations. The given approach not only helps to resolve urgent conflicts but also preconditions constructive future collaboration so that all the parties can feel that they are valued and respected.

Managing Escalations

Navigating the complexities of negotiation requires a bad understanding of when to escalate talks to higher tiers. It is very important to identify the signals that an up-escalation should be done in order to preserve the continuity and wholesomeness of the negotiations. The rationale indications that may lead to escalation are the persistent stalemate, inability to resolve any issues, and exhaustion of power. Such scenarios require a strategic reaction in order to manage the escalation process as diplomatically as possible.

A tricky issue when it comes to introducing the concept of escalation into a negotiation is delicate. It is important to position the escalation as a positive move as opposed to the failure to agree. Word choice can also be central to this perception; the by-line, It would help to coordinate with my manager or legal team to give their input to ensure that this would be done correctly, is perhaps not as hostile as, It would be nice to confer with my manager or legal team to give input on this so this is done correctly. This strategy assists in ensuring that the relationships are balanced and bridges are not burnt, since this is critical in future relations.

When it comes to an escalation meeting, planning is paramount. It introduces the new parties to the developments of the negotiation to date, as well as the areas of stagnation. This is to eliminate confusion and the feeling of repetition so that each would be on the same page and share the same understanding. An escalation meeting that has been carefully prepared can enhance a more constructive dialogue that could not otherwise be realized.

Emotions in escalation meetings are very high, and sometimes they explode. There must be a plan for defusing the situation in case the situation turns hot. Employ phrases like, I feel that we all have some excitement about this, but maybe we could take a minute and come back with some new ideas, to cool things down and get the group back on track. All the parties should be reminded of common goals and see whether there is such a ground before further intensification.

The presence of a higher authority in the process of negotiation not only involves decisions but also the introduction of objective opinion into the discussion that may assist in revealing new resolutions. They will be able to provide ideas and options that were not thought of before, and potentially give them the room to resolve the issue. Their involvement demands a brief overview of the problems in question, as well as any former efforts to solve them. This preparation will help make sure the escalation is constructive and is aimed at finding the solution instead of rekindling old fights.

Efficient escalation management is an art capable of changing the course of negotiations. It involves the combination of firmness and tactfulness because the problems must be raised, but at the same time, relationships and prospects must not be damaged. Instead of using escalation as a final resort, by succeeding at treating it as a strategic instrument, negotiators can continue to exercise control over the process and spearhead an outcome that is beneficial to all parties. It is good to learn how to control escalations not only to improve the current negotiation process, but also to develop the basis of trust and respect that could become a priceless asset in further activities.

Chapter 7: Creating Value in Negotiations

Expanding the Pie

The pie-expanding mentality breaks the universal pattern in negotiations of antagonistic pursuance by parties to have most of what is available. They no longer have to compete over the pieces of something, which can be thought of as a pre-existing pie, but concentrate on expanding the pie and generating new value that can be distributed among all parties involved. This strategy will not only lead to cooperation but may also reveal other alternatives that could have been lost in a zero-sum game.

Making the pie bigger requires the negotiators first to strive to ascertain the interests and priorities of all the parties concerned, and not just restrict themselves to monetary terms. This entails further digging into the non-monetary motives like timing, recognition, exclusivity, and flexibility. By revealing these items, negotiators will be able to evolve through collaborative brainstorming to come up with more value that will fulfill the larger array of needs and wants.

This concept is practically applied in different industries. As an example, in the technology industry, businesses may provide support or training along with software licenses, thereby increasing the perceived value of an offering. One can also add additional value to both sides by providing benefits such as a public case study or a referral opportunity in the consulting line of business. Freelancers can negotiate flexible due dates in exchange for higher rates, therefore, increasing the size of the pie beyond the scope of the project in question.

The pie-expanding process entails a change in strategy whereby the win-lose thought process is replaced with a win-win mentality. This necessitates the negotiators to use an "expand then divide" approach in which the attention is put first on adding value and then on its division. Some tools can be used, including a visual value matrix to map and rank value drivers on both sides, to help clarify what is most important to each one.

The negotiators can also find creative trade-offs and develop multi-issue proposals by adhering to this course of action. To illustrate, in the process of negotiating a job offer, compensation (salary, title, work-from-home options, professional development opportunities, etc.) may be packaged in a way that pleases both sides of the bargaining table.

Also, the log-rolling approach, which uses minor issues to arrange bigger gains, can be utilized in order to prioritize issues better and obtain maximum benefits. This requires the structuring and presentation of multi-issue proposals so that the two parties can test and modify trade-offs via the use of "what-if" proposals to ensure the final agreement represents a balanced and fair division of the expanded pie.

The ultimate objective of pie expansion is to maneuver concessions without losing power. Negotiators are advised to use strategic timing and sequencing when making concessions, such that any concession made is framed as thoughtful and conditional, as opposed to automatic. This upholds the sense of value on concessions, and thus, premature or one-up agreements are avoided.

By adopting the philosophy of pie expansion, negotiators not only have a better chance of getting good deals but also create better long-standing relationships based on mutual respect and shared prosperity. This will change the nature of negotiations and turn them into a cooperative effort where the aim is to create value and to form long-term relationships.

Creative Trade-Offs

The most important factor in the course of negotiation strategy is the capability to be creative in balancing the bargains. This includes the development of multi-issue offers so that the two sides can find a beneficial exit. The idea of this strategy is that it helps to find out some specific problems and combine them into one package, which enlarges the range of the discussion. This approach not only increases the prospects of achieving a desirable agreement but also creates a friendlier environment.

When building a negotiation package, it is imperative to incorporate a diversity of issues that can be negotiated at once. This can include things such as the salary, title, working remotely, or professional development opportunities during a discussion of a job offer. Through expanding the agenda, negotiators can afford to focus on areas of greatest interest and trade on the less costly, high-value items to ensure that each party gets what they feel is important. This, what is generally termed as logrolling, is used when a party gives access to less important matters in order to access more important aspects elsewhere.

A distinct organizational pattern of a multi-issue proposal and its presentation can effectively augment the given process of negotiations. A sequential model is preferable, as it involves preparing and organizing subsections of the proposal. Employing other tools, such as worksheets or checklists, may help in the organization of the different parts of a proposal, which helps to have the whole proposal covered. Moreover, use the headline with connective words or phrases such as what if..." Alternative scenarios are a valuable tool to test and adjust trade-offs collaboratively and enable negotiators to explore new possibilities without committing to one direction at an early stage.

To illustrate, in a situation where the extension of the contractual period may result in the addition of an extra rate on a monthly basis, a question triggered by a scenario like this can open up a discussion that would determine any alteration that would favor both sides. In the same sense, an offer to take on an additional project in exchange for flexi-time can also show a desire to compromise and give good chances of achieving a favourable outcome.

Maneuvering concessions without relinquishing bargaining power is also another skill that is critical to negotiation. Strategic timing and sequencing of concessions should be clear, and there must be diligence in the making of each move. This can be done well by ensuring that concessions are not made two at a time without seeking a payback on the side. Not only does this sustain the perceived value of each concession, but it also invites the temptation of give and take by the other party.

Reconstructing concessions as considerate and purposeful as opposed to innate aids in preserving their usefulness. Phrases like, "Could you do Y like I can do X?" The concession is presented in a wider context of negotiation strategy than the act of a giveaway. The presentation of scripts and frameworks of conditional concessions can help negotiators in keeping balance and control in the discussion.

The idea of drawing creative trade-offs in the process of negotiation goes beyond the point of reaching an agreement. It involves putting in place a structure where several interests can be met so that it can have a more relaxing solution. With the use of such approaches, negotiators will succeed in striking trade-offs in a way that benefits all parties so that none would feel undervalued and misunderstood.

Navigating Concessions

In the context of negotiation, concessions are recurrently viewed as an evil, and concession management is a skill that evinces how strategic an individual is. Negotiating concessions, timing, and sequence may be the key variables in keeping leverage or losing it. This becomes sacrosanct in not making two concessions in succession without a quid pro quo thereof. This is so because by acting in such a manner, every concession will not be seen as an automatic giveaway but as a considerate act on the part of each complex party.

It is vital to frame the concessions. Negotiators can take advantage of conditional language by saying, If I can offer you this, could you give me the middle ground on that? Negotiators can still be seen to be offering as much as they can afford to lose. This not only protects their bargaining, but also creates reciprocal behaviour, thus making the negotiation healthier.

A useful weapon in this Renaissance armoury is the concession ledge, a manoeuvring programme for giving and taking. By noting every concession and the reciprocating payoff, negotiators are able to keep a clear picture of the direction in which the negotiation is heading and hence are not tempted or under pressure to give more out of their resources than required.

Concessions that are premature or a one-sided tendency are very dangerous. They may cause a misplaced loss of leverage and even unfavorable terms. Now, the situation might arise that one has over-conceded. Then, too, there is the way of recovery. Returning to past adaptations and putting them in the context of greater aims, the negotiators get a chance to neutralize the proceedings and make sure that the results are win-win.

In setting up this-for-that agreements, cognizance of the quid pro quo arrangements is achieved when the mechanics of opposing bargaining are recognized. These agreements are important since they create trust and fairness, which decreases the bitter feelings and promotes collaboration. The offer of give-to-get must be explained clearly, which is obvious since otherwise, everyone may get confused and lose a sense of mutual profitability.

The best practices that should be observed in this area are that any mutual agreements should be written down and makes the agreements to be confirmed. Regardless of email templates or in the language of a contract, clarity in communication helps all parties remain on the same page without creating possible issues throughout the entire process.

The strategies have varied usage in relation to a professional setting. In other situations, such as a start-up, equity can be offered in exchange for an advisory role with a view to building long-term partnerships. In a law firm, a discount fee may be tendered in lieu of a client's referral promise, hence forming a symbiotic relationship.

In the end, negotiating concessions should not only be about making news but about the formulation of a mutually advantageous pattern of relations. Negotiators can achieve stronger, more resilient agreements by approaching concessions with strategic intent and clarity, in order to turn potential weaknesses into an asset. Such a careful appreciation of concession enables an embarker to not only gain what he wants in the immediate time but also to set in place the foundations of prolonged professional relationships.

Quid Pro Quo Structuring

Reciprocal bargaining has been used in negotiation to mean that there is an exchange of commitment and benefits between various parties, where there is a balance between the parties involved in any exchange. It is not just a strategy of offering favors in exchange, but one that is based on gaining trust and being fair. The core of this strategy is the principle of a give-to-get in order to minimize anger and establish cooperation, thereby contributing to an easier negotiation session, as well as the implementation of more durable agreements.

When it comes to quid pro quo, details as to what benefits the two parties will beget and what counterparts will be made available should be easily articulated. By making their offers explicit in terms of their reciprocity, negotiators will be able to reduce the misunderstandings and encourage a collaborative climate. Take, for example, a scenario where one party may offer prompt payment to the other party in the event that the delivery may be accelerated. Through such transparent communication, expectations can be made and understandings sealed.

It is important to document these agreements in order to avoid some misinterpretations. The right documentation acts as a point of reference and assists in maintaining clarity during the negotiation. Self-serving advice is that templates or special contract language can help to capture these reciprocal arrangements. This makes both parties agree on what has been settled on, thereby lowering the chances of disagreement in the future.

Quid pro quo strategies may also be applied between industry-specific contexts, which further manifests the versatility and effectiveness of the strategy. In a startup setting, equity-based compensation of advisors can create common ground and incentivize growth. Similarly, law firms can offer fee discounts in exchange for referrals, which would increase their client base and make them profitable.

Quid pro quo agreements are only enhanced in effectiveness when they have been used with the right context and the needs of the industry and parties involved. This needs insightful knowledge of the value proposition of either party, as well as the priorities of the other party. When negotiators make offers that match what is most valued by the other party, they will make proposals that are difficult to resist.

In order to explain these proposals, it is important to use professional language, which would demonstrate confidence and clarity. The practical (business) examples can be useful, giving an outline of both small-stakes and large-stakes negotiations. When giving an exclusive deal, a negotiator may say, "Assuming you can commit to this partnership, today we can offer you an exclusive discount." These assertions not only require the mutuality of the agreement but also add urgency to the decisions as soon as possible.

In addition to this, some of the best practices in the confirmation of such agreements should be highlighted. This also involves the adoption of email templates or particular contract provisions that clearly define the terms of the quid pro quo agreement. This helps to keep both parties in agreement and a commitment to the terms that they have agreed on to eliminate any disagreement in the future.

The whole idea of quid pro quo structuring is to create an atmosphere in which both sides feel cared for and treated fairly. It can be a valuable asset in negotiations in situations where the negotiators are aiming at long-lasting relationships founded on trust and win-win advantages. When practicing the techniques of reciprocal bargaining, the professionals can ensure a better result in their negotiation, which can guarantee a successful and long-lasting business relationship.

Chapter 8: Building Long-Term Relationships

Trust and Rapport Techniques

Being able to establish trust and rapport in professional negotiations, as quickly as possible, is an essential skill in a fast-moving world. In situations where time can be of the essence when negotiating, professionals can ensure they master the art of connection that will drastically change their potential adversarial interaction to a collaborative process. One starts to create rapport by first engaging properly-- motivated small talk and honest compliments that the other person will appreciate. The acknowledgement of commonality of interests or experience is a bond that bridges the gap, leading to a climate of mutual respect and understanding.

One more powerful technique of creating rapport is mimicking and matching words and communication patterns. This can be done by adjusting the tone, pace, and words used in a subtle manner that does not interrupt the style used by the other party. In doing so, the negotiators are able to build a sense of familiarity, thus easing the interactions. Such convergence in communication can really diminish the perceived distance between parties and move negotiations in a fluent and friendly direction.

Trust has a strong turbo effect through transparency. Greater openness of goals, intentions, and concerns promotes openness in reciprocity by the other party. This openness may be laced with strategic vulnerability- not only expressing that something is to be accomplished, but also why it is personally or professionally meaningful. Using language such as, What I am interested in achieving and why it is important to me invites the other party involved in the negotiation to view the process not as a win-lose exercise.

Overcoming distrust or doubt is very important in building trust. Brushing off the reservations by telling the other party that you understand their cautious approach, like, "I know you are apprehensive, let us start low and go high," can make a positive difference. This shows understanding and readiness to build trust step by step, not to gain it in advance. This softens the tensions and even prepares the way for more meaningful conversations.

Another strategy that would help build trust would be to focus on the long-term rather than on short-term gains. Such an attitude change entices the negotiators to long-term business, referrals, and reputations rather than instant profits. Professionals can build long-term partnerships that will be valuable in the long term by negotiating with the future in focus. These include tactics such as bargaining over renewal terms and escalation mechanisms that make sure that both parties have a vested interest in sustaining the relationship.

It is vital to resolve the conflicts or differences in ways that maintain the relationship. Adapting to the cooperation method when resolving issues can turn the setbacks into chances to build trust. Statements such as, How are we going to solve this together? Will demonstrate a willingness to work collectively to solve the problem, which can transform an inhospitable negotiation into the basis of a long-term alliance.

It can be concluded that the tools of building trust and rapport in the negotiation do not have a single clear recipe, but rather require blending empathy, considerate communication styles, and long-term relationship-building skills. By using these methods, the negotiators will achieve a mutually collaborative atmosphere that promotes not only the achievement of successful outcomes but also establishes a foundation upon which they may engage in the future.

Negotiating for Partnerships

Negotiation is the most critical element in the complex process of establishing partnerships. It is simply a matter of getting an agreement, but one that is sustainable and creates a mutually beneficial relationship. Negotiating partnerships involves ending that win-lose mindset and developing a more collegiate approach to negotiating where both parties can see the benefit in the partnership.

The key to effective negotiation of a partnership is knowing the fundamental interests of the two parties. It means looking beneath the surface, looking at motivations and needs, and understanding what is moving either party.

Once these interests are discovered, the negotiators can find areas of mutual gain and direct them to the benefit of both parties. This system will build a culture of trust and cooperation- critical to a long-term partnership.

Communication is the key to negotiating partnerships. Straightforward, candid, and transparent communication assists in setting up the expectations and limiting the possibility of miscommunication. It is important to spell out what each party would like to achieve, as well as what they can give. This openness aids in making achievable objectives and it makes sure that both parties will be on the same frequency right at the beginning.

Negotiating partnerships requires the development of rapport and trust. This can also be done by active listening and empathy that focuses on showing interest in the other party's opinion. By listening and by making their concerns feel heard, negotiators can establish a firm platform of trust, which is essential in a good partnership. Building trust does not just happen; it takes time and effort on a regular basis with honesty.

The negotiators ought to think about adding value to both sides. This means exploring ways that will increase the size of the pie and not battle it out over the existing shares. Looking at creative solutions and compromises, disagreement negotiators can tend to increase the value of the partnership in general. This can include combining services, pooling resources, or even coming up with new forms of collaboration that were previously not envisioned.

Partner negotiations require flexibility and adaptability of the negotiator. Changing the strategies and adjusting the tactics to the realities of the situation or to the arrival of new information is very important. Negotiators must be ready to reopen and redesign their offers as the negotiations continue, and continue to serve the emerging needs and objectives of the parties.

The other notable point is the documentation of agreements. A list of clearly written terms can prevent future conflicts and also help the partnership have a point of reference. This also involves drawing lines on the roles, schedules, and means of addressing the possible conflicts. A properly written agreement has the benefit of being a guide on how the partnership should run so as to achieve its set goals.

Lastly, effective negotiations of partnerships acknowledge the merits of managing relationships in the long run. Reaching an agreement is not sufficient since continuation and development of the relationship are also important. Communication, reviewing the partnership on a periodical basis, and willingness to resolve any issues that come up will ensure the partnership is fruitful.

Partnership negotiation is not all about the first transaction. It is about putting the necessary groundwork to facilitate a relationship that is able to evolve and transform with time and create value for all parties. When negotiators meet at the intersection of mutual interests, open communication, trust-building, and flexibility, the relationships created have a long-lasting future.

Handling Mistakes

In negotiation, learners not only make errors, but this is also a part of the learning curve. When they occur, you will probably recoil in embarrassment or frustration. They have the power to turn them into a learning process of improving negotiation skills in the future. A failure in negotiation can provide a special perspective upon which one can evaluate the reasons for what went wrong in the negotiation.

Each error is an indication of a mirror portraying lapses in preparation or performance. It is imperative to change the orientation towards seeing mistakes as a platform for growth and not as a wall. This display inspired a retrospective evaluation of the misstep and the role of understanding the circumstances that currently contribute to the error. Was it a failure to read the intentions of the other party? It may have been an oversight in knowledge assimilation or a lack of understanding of non-verbal actions. Breaking down these elements, the negotiators will be able to single out areas in which they can improve.

Additionally, being able to approach handling mistakes with both humility and resilience is important. Admission of a mistake can be effective in taking the edge off things and in creating confidence. It acts as a show of goodwill to the other side, showing that there is a willingness to be open and right wrongs. This not only rescues the current negotiation but also prepares the terrain for firmer treatments in the coming interactions.

Moreover, errors may serve as a source of improvement for negotiation mechanisms. They have pointed out the requirement of being exceptionally flexible and adaptable. A rigid strategy can easily fail in case of unanticipated obstacles, whereas a fluid mind can make a negotiator change the strategy and revise it on the fly. Such flexibility does not only mean the ability to vary maneuvers but also to reconsider assumptions and be ready to accept new information or opinions.

Besides personal reflection, it will be useful to seek the opinions of trusted colleagues/mentors. There would be things perceived in the given negotiation by other marks that were not visible on the individual side. Critical comments can provide clarity to blind spots and provide new tactics or ways of thinking to use in future negotiations.

Mistakes also stress the importance of preparation and rehearsal. Although every situation is impossible to prepare for, serious preparation will reduce the chances of inaccuracies. Such preparation involves learning about the requirements and limitations of the other party, predicting challenges that may occur, and preparing scenarios on how to respond to different situations. Practising such scenarios with a colleague can lead to confidence and competence in the negotiation, the delivery of which is less likely to be flawed.

The major lesson to be learned when dealing with errors is the building of resilience. Negotiation, like any other practice, comes with experience and practice. Errors are involved in this process as a way to serve as reminders that the absence of perfection is not the objective, but rather a sense of progress. Acceptance of errors as a means to the end helps the negotiators gain more confidence and effectiveness.

In sum, errors in a negotiation cannot be completely avoided, but they can be very valuable. When negotiators manage to see setbacks as a growth and learning experience, they can turn them into stepping stones to becoming a master negotiator. This mentality not only pairs well with the individual abilities but also raises the overall level of negotiations, giving them a more positive and fruitful nature.

Continuous Growth Practices

As communication in the world of negotiation is dynamic, growth should not only be an aim, but also a process of survival in the long run. Negotiation is a skill like any other art that must be constantly evolving, adjusting, and learning. In order to have a course of growth, one must have an open mind that is prone to changes and enhancements. This includes acquiring new strategies and testing and revising previous avenues on a frequent basis.

The promise of continuous self-assessment is one of the cornerstones of continuous growth. This will include taking some time out to remind yourself of the previous negotiations and how some of the strategies fared, as well as some areas that need improvement. Remembering all the negotiations in a detailed form can be a great tool in the process. The main pieces of information that should be described in this log are dates, context, objectives, and results, as well as any remarkable strategic moves. On periodical review of these entries, patterns can be seen, strengths noted, and areas that need development identified.

The second important practice is participation in peer reviews or feedback. Debriefing with trusted peers or mentors can offer new insight and an alternate look at an experience that would not be as obvious when operating alone. These classes can be modeled on certain negotiation situations, and afford focused feedback and discussion. By including different perspectives, negotiators will be in a position to widen their perspective and improve their skills.

It is also important to stay updated with the newest trends and techniques of negotiation in order to grow further. This may be done by reading related material, attending classes, or going online to take courses. Reading new materials and learning new concepts can keep the skills sharp and flexible to the changes in the environment of negotiation. It also develops a sort of proactive knowledge-gathering attitude where negotiators do not just wait to be given knowledge; instead, they can always pursue it.

Besides, it can be said that the process of setting and revising individual goals should be introduced to boost continuous growth. These objectives are supposed to be specific, measurable, attainable, relevant, and time-bound (SMART). Good objectives will help the negotiators concentrate their efforts on attaining some specific outcomes. Periodically evaluating such objectives enables such adjustments to be made when circumstances change or upon an insight that is newer to them because of recent events.

Continuous growth will also imply accepting failure as an opportunity to learn. Not every negotiator is exempt from setbacks, but individuals who believe that failures can help them become better when they see setbacks as stepping stones can use failures as stepping stones toward success. It is fundamental to take some time to reflect on what went wrong, why it happened, and how it can be avoided in the future as a means of ensuring that failure is integrated into lessons learned.

Finally, implementing a growth mindset is an essential consideration for practices of continuous growth. This paradigm focuses on the fact that to improve abilities and become more intelligent, an individual has to be dedicated and hardworking. It promotes rigidity and endurance, which are vital when approaching the obstacles that are bound to be encountered in negotiation. By helping to inculcate this kind of growth mindset, negotiators will be able to stay motivated and driven, even when they find themselves in unfavorable situations.

To conclude, constant development of negotiation is a complex task, which cannot be accomplished without devotion, analysis, and the desire to acquire new knowledge. The ways to become an effective negotiator during self-evaluations, feedback, information gathering, goal setting, failure learning experiences, and a growth mindset may help negotiators continue being effective and successful in their activities.

Chapter 9: Digital Negotiation Strategies

Mastering Video Call Negotiations

In the arena of modern negotiation, the transition into the digital environment created a set of challenges, as well as a new set of possibilities, especially regarding video calls. It is important to impress a commanding presence on screen so that negotiations can run with ease and efficiency. The initial process is developing an executive behavior with the personality of instilling both power and accessibility. This will entail focus on camera angles, light, and background settings that should be professional. Positioning the camera at eye level can produce the feeling of a direct interaction, and the proper lighting can call attention to the facial expressions, which are one of the points of delivering sincerity and transparency.

The space in which these calls would be conducted should be distraction-free; therefore, it is necessary to ensure that the choice of such a space is a quiet room in a well-organized environment. When the meeting takes place in remote environments, professional clothing should be respected as the norm since it establishes the mood of the encounter and creates the gravity of the negotiation.

Rapport-building in a virtual environment takes some effort and strategic communication. Opening meetings with mindful small talk can trigger the ice to melt and the participants to relax in the negotiation game. These will include conversational tricks like referring to names or nicknames commonly to make the conversation personalized, digital body language like nodding or mirroring as a means of conveying a sense of connection, and even understanding. Use check-in questions at the start of meetings, as they also help to create a human connection so that the participants are more open to collaborative discussions.

Video calls. This is an important aspect of negotiating in video calls. Clarity and concise messages help avert miscommunication that tends to scuttle a deal during negotiations. One should recap important agreements verbally over the phone so that the parties can have a shared understanding of the provisions. Screen sharing can also be an effective technique to illustrate a visual demonstration of what may be a complex verbal agreement. It can be used as a confirmation point on a particular selling point.

There is always a possibility that technical problems or communication breakdowns occur during a video call, though every effort is made. Troubleshooting scripts can help to sail through what would otherwise be hiccups. An example of this is when a technical failure has occurred or a participant has dropped off communication, the disruption of the negotiation process or call can be minimized by having a predetermined script to begin with that addresses and manages the disruption. Also, the methods to reintegrate a quiet or non-listening participant, like calling him or her directly or recapping the most important details to grab his or her full attention, are necessary.

The terrain of bargaining has changed fast and dramatically with the introduction of digital communications, and understanding how to negotiate in this new territory is an important key to success. With attention to presence, rapport, and clarity, negotiators will be able to harness video calls to their advantage and guarantee the equal impact and success of digital negotiations compared to face-to-face ones.

Email and Chat Negotiations

The challenges and opportunities of navigating the domain of email and chat negotiations are not similar to more traditional face-to-face interactions in any way. Another major feature of these digital bargains is that they are asynchronous, and this may be a blessing and a curse to communication. Lack of real-time contact also gives negotiators the freedom to contemplate before responding properly because they have time to plan. Yet, the same lack may imply loss of tone and context and thus deprive one of an opportunity to convey any minorities that may be easily revealed face-to-face.

The asynchronous character also introduces challenges related to time zone compatibilities, where communicating parties might not be available at the same time. Thus, a delay in communications can originate, as well as a lack of understanding. Email and chat have, on the other hand, the benefit of documentation. All transactions are registered so that they can be a resourceful source of reference and accountability of the process.

Constructing effective communication when using email and chats during negotiations needs consideration of the tone as well as clarity. The written word does not have the facial expressions or vocal inflections that tend to give particular meaning or tone. Thus, negotiators need to make an effort to communicate through very specific language, which is neutral. Software that analyses the tone of written communication is also handy to make sure what is intended to come out is effectively coming out. Emojis should not be ambiguous or contain sarcasm or humour, as they might be misinterpreted at any time.

Time is the other important factor in email and chat negotiations. Responsiveness of a negotiator can go a long way in determining how the negotiation will proceed. Short turnaround times are a way to communicate a sense of enthusiasm and interest, and delay may imply apathy or a lack of urgency. Development of expectations regarding response time at the early stages can help control these perceptions and keep the negotiation going. Some steps in tackling slow or unresponsive responses would include correspondent follow-ups and reminders that do not come off as pressure but can keep the flow going.

Templates can prove extremely useful in organizing the negotiations by means of email and chat. By preparing in advance models of opening offers, counteroffers, and closing offers, the company will save time and will be able to ensure consistency in such deals. These templates provide a framework that is flexible enough to be adapted in relation to the circumstances of each negotiation process, enabling the negotiators to discuss content and not format.

To conclude, email and chat are challenging media in terms of negotiation, which is why they still have certain advantages that should be utilized to negotiate successfully. Certainly, intentional and effective communication with a particular focus on the time and manner of interaction can help negotiators to tackle this digital environment. Application of temssplates and tone checking tools also supports this effort, so that even in the absence of face-to-face contact, negotiations can be conducted in a professional and yet personable manner, to ensure desired results are realized. With the advent of digital negotiation in our more integrated contemporary world, the need to be adept in these skills has become vital to those people vying to advance their careers.

Templates and Timing

Templates and timing also play an important role in the negotiation world, where a clever deployment of the same can catapult the result of any negotiation. The flexibility and advantage of templates can form the basis of organizing a negotiation, and the timing may improve or worsen the negotiations. The combined effect of these elements constitutes an effective strategy that will enable negotiators to exercise their power and influence the favourable outcomes.

Templates are important as they offer some structure to negotiation. They also provide a sort of guide to follow the discussion and cover all essential points in a step-by-step manner. These frameworks are especially useful in more complex negotiations, in which multiple variables interact. With the help of templates, negotiators become more focused, are able to streamline communication, and prevent pitfalls that often come about due to a lack of structure in a conversation between parties. Templates may be checklist-type or highly scripted depending on the scenarios they are intended to address. An example of a complete checklist could have major objectives, possible concessions, and backup points. In contrast, a script could consist of specific words to use in opening and replying to points.

The malleability of the templates enables them to fit within the peculiarities of each negotiation. This flexibility is vital because there is no equal negotiation. The list of factors, like industry norms, cultural ones, and personal styles of bargaining, requires a customized approach. Negotiators can develop tailor-made templates in advance and, thus, prepare possible issues and appropriate counter-arguments, increasing their preparedness and confidence.

Time, however, is the delicate know-how of when to do things and when to wait. It consists of keeping negotiating temperature gauged, as to when to provide new information, concessions, or other details that can lead to the closure. When these actions are taken, there can be a far-reaching impact on the flow of the negotiation. For example, it is possible to open a significant concession too early so as to devalue it, and it is also possible not to open it soon enough so as to lose leverage.

Effective timing also concerns the ability to see the mechanisms and beats of the negotiation process. This involves a realization of when the other party is most open, when he or she may require time to absorb information, and when he or she is likely to agree on a point. Experienced negotiators will be able to read these signs and fine-tune their tactics to meet these changes. The techniques they use include the strategic pause that gives time to think, and in most cases can make the other party fill the pause with concessions or other valuable information.

In addition, timing can also be applied in the larger scope of the negotiation, which would involve market timing or organizational urgency that can affect the decision-making process of the other party. Evaluating the mayhem around them helps negotiators to ensure that the timing of their offerings is the best they can be.

In conclusion, templates and timing are both valid strategies that can be included in the system of negotiation with the view of attaining desirable results. Templates provide the structure and clarity you need to broach a complicated discussion, and the subtle use of timing helps you to sway how the negotiation is progressed. Combined, they are a strategic negotiating toolkit that enables negotiators to evolve with each interaction individually by being prepared, having flexibility, and entering each conversation with greater confidence to achieve more sustainable and more successful agreements.

Virtual Checklists

In today's busy, competitive world of negotiations, virtual checklists have become a must-have tool in terms of ensuring thorough preparations and flawless implementation. Being in the form of checklists, these digital companions will guide the negotiators through the difficulties of both online and face-to-face negotiations. These checklists ensure that an effective negotiation is composed of all the various components that make it successful, and ensure that all the components are well organized.

The most important feature of virtual checklists is the possibility of adjusting and tailoring them to a particular context of negotiation. They are not fixed; they are live templates that generate with every negotiation encounter. Professionals should develop their own checklists according to their business needs and individual negotiation profiles. This customization makes the checklists timely and useful since it assures the negotiators that he/she cannot miss something important.

A virtual checklist is well-designed since it encompasses a wide scope of actions to prepare. The initial step is a robust check of the technology to ensure that all digital technology, software, and devices are performing as well as possible. This involves piloting video conferencing software, maintaining a reliable internet connection, and checking on any presentation materials. These measures beforehand are essential to the prevention of technical glitches that might hamper the progress of the negotiations.

In addition to technical aspects, virtual checklists underline the necessity of psychological preparedness. Negotiators are further advised to think about negotiations in advance, which might involve preparation of prior key points to negotiate, problems that might arise during the negotiation, and rehearsing responses to different situations. Such a process of mental priming is important to remain calm and flexible in response to unexpected events.

Body language, despite being more difficult to detect in a virtual environment, is an essential part of any good communication. Virtual checklists also remind the negotiators to be conscious of their online body language, e.g., eye contact with the camera and using gestures to illustrate points. They also act as a reminder to be keen on the body language of counterparts, even in a virtual environment, in order to detect reactions and to change strategies accordingly.

Another addition within the virtual checklists is follow-up plans. They make sure that the negotiation process does not stop at the first meeting, but by organizing different follow-ups. This involves setting up follow-up meetings, writing up agreements signed, and having open channels of communication for any arising problems. This conscientiousness assists in cementing deals and long-term contacts within the working world.

Furthermore, the virtual checklists are confidence enhancers. With a properly described path consisting of various tasks and objectives, the negotiators can enter the discussion with more confidence, knowing that they have what it takes to deal with the situation. Such self-belief is also usually manifested in their attitudes and may have a positive impact in negotiation.

Fundamentally, virtual checklists are not only organizational tools but also strategic necessities that enable negotiators to perform optimally. With this set of thoroughly constructed guides to their craft integrated into their negotiating processes and practices, even the most complex aspects of modern-day negotiations will prove far more navigable with a far higher chance of success.

Chapter 10: Psychological Tactics

Spotting Manipulation

The more intricate the negotiation dance, the better one's ability to sniff out manipulation early on is, like a sixth sense. It is a crucial skill that has the capacity to turn a potentially dangerous situation into one that gives space for clarity and truth. Today, manipulative tactics are widespread in negotiations and can vary in severity, subtleness, and reach all the way to guilt-tripping and gaslighting. It is these maneuvers that should be recognized before you start being able to counter them effectively.

Guilt-tripping can be considered the initial step in the manipulation of the negotiation. This is done so that the other party will feel that they are to blame for something they are not, to a decision that benefits the manipulator. Another common strategy is gaslighting, which in this case involves one party trying to make the other question his or her perception or understanding of what is happening. This may leave a feeling of discomfort and misunderstanding, which eventually results in bad decision-making.

Another manipulative ploy that is commonly employed is false urgency. It is also engaged in building up a feeling of pressure to make a decision and be hurried up, usually by false deadlines or exaggeration of what happens when one does not take that decision. This may create excessive pressure and result in rash decision-making, which might not reflect the best interests of a person. Using the same procedure, the 'divide and conquer' method aims at severing the connections between an individual and the support structures, thus making them prone to manipulation.

Being able to identify such tactics requires sharp observation skills, both verbal and non-verbal. Such behavioral cues as passing blame, over-flattery, or giving out information are major clues that one is manipulative. Verbal signals may be discrepancies in the story of the other party or the requirements that change unexplainably over a period of time. Such short changes, especially without any explanations given, are a sure indicator of some manipulation.

The most effective way of dealing with these tactics is to employ an aggressive questioning strategy. Questions such as, Can you explain how you came to this deadline? These are not only questions that contradict the manipulative narrative, but they are also questions that foster openness. Taping discussions and asking for third-party confirmation is an extra tool that can be used to ground negotiations on the realities and keep the other party accountable so that he/she cannot renegotiate or dish out new terms.

It is important to stay calm when dealing with manipulation. The point is to overcome the issue diplomatically in order to maintain the level of professionalism and credibility. Framing, like letting us look at the facts and figures, and what both of us can agree upon, can assist in getting the dialogue back into a positive dimension.

The capacity to identify manipulation is not just about ensuring self-protection, but about the creation of a negotiating environment where both parties can negotiate sincerely. By becoming aware of manipulators and outsmarting them, market participants are capable of preserving the integrity of the negotiation process and creating outcomes that are fair and justified by all parties. This alertness and readiness give negotiators the confidence and clarity that help them negotiate complex relations.

Emotion Management

Emotion management is one of the core aspects in the process of negotiation, as situations of high stakes generate emotion-intensive reactions. The skill in being able to negotiate successfully in such emotional waters may determine successful negotiators and those who are less successful at it. Improving their knowledge of neuroscience behind emotional contagion and the role of mirror neurons would give them a basic understanding of why emotions can so easily spread through a negotiation and influence the other in the process.

One of the essentials in the management of emotions is the ability to know how one responds emotionally and to control it. These include practices like name it to tame it, in which people express their emotions so as to take control of them. Labeling or naming emotions, whether it's frustration, anxiety, or excitement, can help the negotiators start to move out of the immediacy of the emotions. Such detachment is also enabled through tactical breathing patterns and emotional-distance exercises and practices to form a barrier against action impulses and enable more deliberate thinking.

Besides dealing with personal emotions, the successful negotiator has to be effective in decoding and responding to the cues of the other person. This will require an acute awareness of micro-expressions, voice modifications, and other such non-verbal signals that may indicate a change in mood. Likewise, defensive posture or a raised tone of voice may be crucial clues that the other party is in the soup. Even when negotiators are not conscious of them as they happen, they can take such signals into account later to modify their strategy, possibly by slowing their tempo, or reassure them to de-escalate matters.

Another thing that should be given to a negotiator is the language and scripts to de-escalate the emotionally charged negotiations. Terms such as I understand that this means something to you, why not take a breather let us check what the alternatives are or set a time to reconvene when we both have settled down can be used to calm things down and create an atmosphere of collaboration. The strategies are available to recognize the feelings of the other party and get the discussion back on course.

In addition, management of emotions can be carried over to the next negotiation encounter, and the negotiators may opt to think about their encounters after the encounter. In this reflection, it will be necessary to analyze what emotional triggers were there, how they were handled, and how the following negotiations may be conducted. This self-assessment is not just good for propelling an individual to a higher state of personal development; it also helps him react better to such situations in the future.

The role of emotion management can not be overestimated in the process of negotiation. It not only makes interactions smoother, but also helps to achieve more desirable results since the decisions should be guided by logic and strategy instead of emotional impulse. With a little practice, the ability to control personal emotions and those of other people can turn a contentious situation into a negotiating tactic that leads to successful and long-lasting agreements.

Leverage Points

In the world of negotiation, leverage points are the under-credited gates that can open great avenues. These do not necessarily concern applying power; on the contrary, they require the unraveling of the invisible influences that can swing the odds in your favor. Leverages come out of many areas, including unique skills, timely frequency, established contacts, adaptability, or the availability of information that no one seems to know.

A careful audit of personal and organizational strengths should be done before approaching any negotiation because of the critical role played by leverage in negotiation. This is relying on what proprietary capabilities you possess, i.e., what you can do that no one and/or other firms can, i.e., being the only supplier that can fulfil a short deadline, or having a long existing relationship with a key stakeholder that other firms may not possess. By plotting out these secret advantages, you can effectively posture yourself during negotiations in such a way that you show off to the other party rather visibly, but in a shrewd and very subtle way, demonstrating the position of strength that you find yourself in.

The essential method of activating leverage is the use of the so-called Theilingmentals. Such an approach requires offering conditional propositions that outline the advantages of the cooperation. An example of this would be saying, "Provided you are committed to this delivery schedule, then we can maintain the premium support through the project". The other tactic is to cite instances of third-party standards or testimonies that support your claim as a potential partner.

It is important to be in a position to pivot when the other party underestimates your position of leverage. This may include subtle reminders of what you are good at, the introduction of new aspects to the discussion, or a rephrasing of the conversation to shift to the positive about you. Another example is showing one of its alliances at the point when the deal is jeopardized, and this may alter the power balance during the negotiation.

Silence, too, is a role that can be effectively employed in the process of negotiation. The strategic pause is also referred to as the silence, and this can also be applied in restoring control and compelling the other party to make concessions or even disclose more information. Psychological effects of silence can usually force the other party to break the silence. In some instances, they can provide more information or even give out the offers that had not come to mind initially. It is, however, advisable to apply this strategy sparingly so as to avoid tendencies to be disengaged.

The other part of capitalizing on negotiation points is to identify the presence of secret agendas. These usually contain silent restrictions or personal motivators that are able to alter the actions of the other party, aligning the interests. Together with the use of probing techniques, it will be possible to uncover these latent desires through the use of indirect questioning. Examples of how to accomplish this include the questions, "What does a positive result look like to you?" or "Can you tell me of any internal imperatives I should know about?"

Most importantly, the use of leverage is meant to bring forth a scenario where both parties benefit optimally. It entails not only the element of exerting pressure but also broadening the options of both parties so that the negotiation is not only a win-or-lose situation but a win-win situation. By learning and making effective use of those leverage points, a negotiator can change the possible conflict into a field of collaboration and value.

Behavioral Economics

When it comes to the subject of negotiation, the concepts of behavioral economics have deep implications for how human psychology is applied in negotiation processes. There is no doubt that these principles are not only academic but also crucial in enabling people to influence the outcomes in their personal and professional negotiations effectively.

The anchor effect is one of the basic principles of behavioral economics. The principle captures how a non-final estimate or figures can have a disproportionate effect on later judgments/decisions. Immediately when entering negotiations, whatever figures that are initially quoted on either side tend to define the entire negotiation process implicitly. As an example, when a seller makes an initiating bid that is high, it can have the effect of guiding the expectations of the buyer so that consequent offers, which would otherwise be objectionably low, can be relatively acceptable in his or her mind. Mastering the concept of anchors and being strategic in its setting can thus be a very useful device in making sure that negotiations start at a positive bias.

Loss aversion is another important concept that explains that people are more willing to avoid losses than to gain equivalent benefits. This could be used to their advantage during negotiations, and they can make offers whenever it is in terms of loss rather than gain. One example is that it can be more effective to focus on what a counterpart will risk missing by failing to seal a deal than on the rewards of agreement. This is playing on the human fear of loss, and this is usually a stronger motivator than the reward of gain.

The endowment effect also explains how possession makes an item appear to us as being more valuable. This may be especially applicable to negotiations that deal with material assets or products. Some parties, when negotiating, will put an asset in the view that it is something that the counterparty already possesses, using this strategy to increase its perceived value in an attempt to get them to accept terms that help them keep the asset.

Reciprocity is a well-documented behavioral tendency, and it has a key role in negotiations. People are psychologically disposed to reciprocate favors given and can be exploited by giving little concessions at the early stages of negotiation. This move may push a suitable feeling of obligation on the other party to pay back, which may lead to a more positive result.

It is also through framing effects that negotiation dynamics are influenced. The perception and choice of decisions can be changed by the way the information is presented. An example is using the idea that a proposal is a time-sensitive offer that can create a sense of urgency and make people make fast decisions. On the same note, presenting the positive side of a deal and downplaying the negative side of a deal can render the offer more appealing.

There is also caution about typical cognitive biases that would sabotage a negotiation strategy, according to behavioral economics. Confirmation bias, where people put more value on the information that adheres to their prior perspectives, can cause negotiators to overlook useful information. In the same vein, excessive confidence may produce the misperception of the opposite side or an assumption that the other side will overvalue its own initiative and thus translate to a strategic mistake.

In order to be successful in applying these principles in negotiations, it is necessary to practice the theories through exercises and scenarios that enable the theories to be practically applied. This may involve role-play sessions, allowing the negotiators a chance to rehearse how to frame concessions as a bonus, or how they can counter their own biases, which could affect both sides of an upcoming negotiation. These kinds of practices not only improve negotiation skills but also enrich the knowledge of how behavioral economics can be put into consideration in order to attain the required results.

Chapter 11: Real-World Scenario Playbooks

Salary Negotiation Scripts

Salary negotiation is a combination of preparation, confidence, and savvy communication. It all starts with knowing that what you contribute to the table is not just how many numbers, but the value and what you have accomplished to deserve the request. Before going into a negotiation, it is important to position your value suggestion in a way that clearly explains what you want and why you deserve it. This takes into account the things that you will bring to the table in terms of revenue or efficiency, and uses market research sources to shore up your demands to industry norms.

The opening script establishes the tone when you commence a salary negotiation, whether via a written medium, such as an email, or in person. In digital form, a template may start with a thank-you to the occasion and a brief outline of what you would like to get along with concrete achievements. As an example, you can begin with, "I appreciate this time to talk about my position and contributions. Following my increased results in client engagement by 25%, I would like to discuss a salary change, which could incorporate such an effect." This plan is not only about mentioning the numbers but also about analyzing your accomplishments in the discussion.

Face-to-face or virtual meetings are more dynamic. The opening statement that has a positive impact needs to state your achievements confidently. Again, "I am looking forward to displaying how I have worked on my recent projects to make our team successful, and how this translates into my current remuneration." Not only does this frame your request in terms of win-win, but it also invites discussion of your role and the contribution you can make in the future.

Objections are a part and parcel of salary negotiations. Employers may react to financial constraints and time-related problems. When such discussions arise, prepared scripts can be used as well, i.e., reacting to budget issues with, I am aware that budgets are not high, however, I believe that I have contributed greatly to our expansion, and I would want to see some way to reflect that." This line reflects the position, but also moves the discussion back to your value.

When an employer proposes to discuss this again later, a wise answer would be, I understand the issues of time. Would you mind scheduling a follow-up meeting to re-evaluate when budget reviews take place?" The reason this keeps the discussion open is that it shows you are willing to work within their limits as well as stand by your side.

The final stage must be a definite confirmation of agreed terms after negotiation. Whether it is an oral agreement or an email reminding them afterwards, this way around, clarity and responsibility will exist. A sample follow-up can be found here. Thank you for the talk we had today. We decided on a salary adjustment, subject to review of the budget. I am excited to give further contributions to the success of the team." This not only puts in black and white the agreement but also makes you feel stronger when it comes to future success.

The most valuable script in the salary negotiations is not a higher ask; instead, it is an articulation of your value to both your desires and those of the organization. Having such discussions ready with clear and value-driven scripts empowers you to hold such discussions with confidence and clarity.

Handling Aggressors

The other situation that has been witnessed with regard to negotiations is finding aggressive counterparts. Aggressors have the capacity to disturb the normal flow of any negotiations, especially during boardrooms, virtual meetings, and even during a non-formal meeting, creating an atmosphere full of tension. Knowledge on how best to handle such scenes is pertinent in ensuring that the discussions remain under control and that they are able to take them in the right direction.

Power tactics employed by aggressors are always aimed at winning or controlling, and can include things like interfering with the speaker to interject, speaking louder, or using the ultimatum. Such behaviors have the propensity to destabilize even the most experienced negotiators, resulting in frustrations and even the crumbling of the negotiation process. Nevertheless, by adopting effective steps, the negotiators can counter these tricks and remain on top.

The preliminary measure in dealing with aggressors is to define limits. The most important thing is assertiveness; one should clearly and calmly state that interruptions will not be allowed. In such a case as frequent interruptions, a negotiator may feel the need to express, "I would like to be able to complete my thought first, then we can proceed." This also affirms control and reports back to the aggressor that its ways will ultimately be fruitless in derailing the process.

The other good strategy is to respond with assertive redirection. It entails redirecting attention to the agenda of discussion and not letting oneself be bamboozled by the antics of an aggressor. Phrases that work well here include the likes of "Let us concentrate on the issues and not the personalities involved". It is also useful as a tension-diffusing tactic because the discussion remains focused on goals instead of skills.

In situations when aggressors are using take-it-or-leave-it language, responding curiously will help instead of resisting. The examples of questions are as follows: Can you assist me with grasping the rationale of that position? What are the data tophi inch homej``禾 Robinson? What data do you support this approach? Not only do they present more information, but they also compel the aggressor to explain his or her position. This may frequently result in a more even-handed discussion since it removes the idea of confrontation.

There are circumstances when, regardless of all the efforts, it is necessary to put a negotiation on hold. Taking a break helps de-escalate emotions to allow time to recompose. This must be done without loss of ground, and phrases like the following should be used: "Let us step back and consider what has already been said." Such a break can be used as a reset opportunity so that all players have a chance to come back with a better focus and enthusiasm.

Eventually, dealing with aggressors is a topic of self-respect and graciousness under duress. Through such approaches, the negotiators are in a position to convert potentially antagonistic relationships into a point of making positive interactive conversations. This maintains the integrity of the negotiation and even increases the chances of attaining a mutually pleasant outcome. In such a way, negotiators can save their interests as well as create a reputation as resilient and composed in adverse situations. These skills are worth their weight in a negotiation table, and can help even the most difficult of situations be negotiated calmly and with assertiveness.

Vendor Negotiations

In the subtlety of vendor negotiations, it is common that the bargaining of prices ceases to be the point and turns to the synchronization of the relationship between vendors, a mutually beneficial and sustainable relationship. The value that a vendor can offer goes deeper than the price, so the art of negotiating with the vendors is based on this understanding. The discussions between you and the vendors then need to shift to incorporating a broader perspective, i.e., they should also include delivery schedules, post-sales services, and possible relationships with the supplier in the long term.

When initiating the negotiation process, the dialogue mustn't merely serve transactional purposes but, more importantly, discuss the larger picture of what both sides can actually do together. This requires an in-depth knowledge of the strengths of that vendor and how these can best be utilized within the context of your organizational objectives. Presenting negotiations in terms of value instead of cost provokes the possibility of creative solutions, which can give rise to the added value as bundled services or extended warranties.

A strategic approach is achieved by being well prepared prior to taking an action. This preparation entails gaining knowledge about where the vendor lies, where their competitive strengths are, and what their limitations are. By noting these areas, you will be able to adjust your negotiation strategy accordingly, using areas where the vendor can have more flexibility. An example is a vendor who may be interested in growing their presence in the market; they may be willing to provide better terms in the form of a long-term contract or a case study collaboration.

During the negotiation, the communications must be clear and effective. This is not just stating what your needs and limitations are, but will also mean clearly listening to the suggestions and objections made by the vendor. These two-way communication helps create a synergistic environment where both parties feel appreciated and understood, and set the path towards a win-win resolution.

When developing proposals, attempt to use frameworks that are innovative and accommodating. Offer win-win solutions that can satisfy the needs of both parties, i.e., restructuring the payment terms or delivery schedules to comply with the capabilities of the vendor rather than altering your business requirements. The method not only contributes towards the achievement of goals during the negotiation process, but also prepares the way or foundation for a sound business relationship in the future.

Communication channels need to be kept open to ensure that both parties stick to the terms agreed, as it is sometimes not easy to get around. Periodic meetings can assist in solving the problem at an early stage and strengthen the alliance. This is also a chance to renegotiate any new conditions that have arisen as the business relationship develops.

Last, write down all agreements. Proper documentation eliminates misunderstanding and ensures clear promises to both sides. It supports going back to the reference point, in case discrepancies arise therein, ensuring the integrity and trust developed in the course of the negotiation process.

Vendor negotiations can be turned into a strategic partnership instead of a strict transactional one when approached with long-term value creation in mind. Such a change of world-view not only leaves the immediate products of the negotiation better off but also leads to the durable success and development of both negotiators.

The No, But Technique

Reflecting the sensitive nature of the art of negotiation, there can be a need to straddle the fine line between aggressiveness and tactfulness. One of the most effective strategies in the dance is the so-called No, But technique, which enables it to decline the requests but continue the positive flow of the discussion. It is an approach that is supposed to cushion the blow of a refusal in such a way that, though an immediate request will be declined, the conversation will stay positive and moving forward.

The gist of this No, But technique is somewhere between establishing limits and never severing the bonds. It is also a means of saying no, though in such a way that does not give an impression of closing the door as such, as it does to the side, so that the conversation steers towards finding other solutions. In this, the relationships are maintained, and the creativity and collaboration in seeking a mutually agreeable solution are promoted.

Primarily, the No, But technique may be used in a variety of scripts corresponding to different situations. In the case of scope creep in a project, one would respond, "No, I cannot stretch out the completion as proposed, but I can prioritize certain activities in order to meet the deadline." This is not only a refusal to the original request but rather an alternative that would keep the project on course.

The psychological reasoning behind the technique lies in the fact that it makes the denial softer. With the expression of the word "no" and instantly after it with an expression of "but," the speaker offers a positive way ahead, therefore limiting the opportunity of conflict or dissatisfaction. The style is an approach that takes into account the needs and concerns of the other party as a sign of willingness to listen and cooperate instead of rejecting immediately.

The technique of No, But has its nuances that can be grasped only with references to the language and time factors. The wording used must be respectful, and the time of response must be such that it is not perceived to be rude and uncomfortable. This is a technique that can be practiced in minor-stakes negotiations to gain confidence and competence; therefore, it is constructive when applied in real, serious negotiations.

Further, it is simple enough to apply the No, But technique even beyond business negotiations in general. Dealing with conflicts of schedules with family or meeting the expectations of friends, this method can be used to bring peace to everyone involved and to have everyone feel that they have been listened to.

The advantage of the No, But method is that it is flexible and can be applied across the board. It also asks what negotiators can do to work around immediate rejections and see beyond them to a wider range of options to advantage all.

Maintaining a constructive and positive attitude can open space in which new solutions can be created; overall, this will result in more successful and satisfying results for all.

In short, the art of No, But is a skill everyone should learn in a bid to improve his/her negotiation arsenal. It not only enables people to defend their boundaries but also creates an environment of mutual respect and cooperation. The more experienced such negotiators are in this approach, the more well-suited they will be to face the challenges of a current interaction, a conflict being an opportunity to improve rather than a dramatic event

Chapter 12: Closing and Following Up

Closing the Deal

It is during this ultimate scene of negotiation that one is mesmerized by how all the strands can come together to form a tapestry of agreement and affirmation. As the conversation progresses, it is vital to identify the small cues that will tell you they are ready to close. These cues, both verbal and nonverbal, are the guiding needle that enables negotiators to reach a successful closure. It can be a nod, a contemplative what next, or a high-fashion yes-yes, it does not matter, as they are all the invitations that the deal is ready to be closed.

The cues do not always indicate readiness. Indecisions are expressed as indefinites or the lapse of dialogue, accompanied by a body language change. Appreciating these opportunities is also essential because they would allow people to discuss nagging doubts or discrete anxieties. Maintaining the right balance between advancing and recalibrating the course.

In this scenery, scripts turn out to be such useful equipment. The confirmation, "Are we all in agreement on these terms?" or a statement that summarizes the next steps that should be taken in order to align, can help to strengthen the mutual understanding and commitment. The art of closing applies not only to face-to-face conversations but also to digital negotiations, where things such as the subtle art of email or manually signing off on an e-signature can be used to finalize deals in the modern world quickly and effectively.

Digital confirmations are the new handshakes that produce the feeling that one is obliged. A detailed email that follows up on a verbal agreement that includes all the terms precisely serves to formalize the agreement and prevent a backtracking situation. The agency of the tools, such as DocuSign, appreciates one factor as formal; closure is handled with considerable security.

Language of closure signals tribunal completeness, but it is also a terminative language that concludes agreements with the possibility of adding whatever clarifications are the final desires. Examples of this would include words like: To clarify, we are both going to commit to... Now, do we need to add or mention anything before bringing this to an end? It should help create an atmosphere of honesty and trust.

Clarity and accountability thrive on documentation. It is important to have immediate written documentation of any agreement, thus avoiding miscommunication and establishing expectations. Clear and concise templates and summaries aligned to the complexity of the deal will make sure that everyone is on the same side of the boat. Whether by bullet points to be easy to understand or by formal papers in case of complicated contracts, one aims to cover all the details with exactness.

It is as vital as the production of such documents to distribute them as well. Receipt confirmation and availability by digital means, such as online cloud data storage, online project management tools, etc, adds transparency and accessibility. This can be done by inserting simple lines like, "Please acknowledge by responding to this email," to strengthen the agreement and the conditions of that purchase.

Once the deal is done, business does not end; it becomes a period of follow-up and development. Active participation also avoids the deterioration of commitments and, therefore, ensures the duties are realized. Scripts such as follow-up, Thank you so much for being a great partner--Here is our agreed-upon timeline, and the next steps will keep the momentum flowing and reinforce the relationship.

Post-agreement problems, such as delays, scope adjustments, and cold feet, must be handled with care and delicate touches, as well as reinstatements. Win-win Negotiation of minor terms where possible will maintain the deal intact, and follow-up should be seen as a bridge to the next deal, as it can lead to a succession and growth of the relationship beyond the particular transaction at hand.

Documenting Agreements

Documentation of agreements is a key practice in the world of professional negotiation to bring about a balance of understanding, accountability, and clarity. The careful procedure of turning the oral promises into the written acts not only helps to safeguard the interests of all the parties involved, but also becomes the source of future references to acts.

There is no overemphasis on the relevance of prompt documentation. It serves as a protection against misunderstandings and miscommunications that may occur sometimes as a result of informal verbal agreements. By offering the terms in a transparent written statement, all the parties will be able to align their expectations and duties and prevent the possibility of disagreement. This positioning is paramount because it creates a base of trust and transparency; these two terms are crucial to any successful working relationship.

To seamlessly conduct this process, it is advisable to use a template and structured summaries. Templates present a structured approach when it comes to recording the essential aspects of an agreement, which include the coverage of the agreement, deliverables, schedule, and roles. Such fill-in-the-blank types of forms will help to preclude any important information being omitted, which will add to the accuracy and thoroughness of the documentation. With more complicated negotiations with numerous stakeholders, more formal documents may be required in order to flesh out the details of the agreement.

The decision (to use bullet-point summaries or formal documents) is made according to the complexity of the agreement and the preferences of the parties involved in it.

Bullet-point summaries are a brief and easy-to-follow option to outline essential things that can come in handy in any less formal setting or in general agreements that are non-sophisticated. Conversely, witnessing: Formal documents have more detail, and they are legally binding—this is critical in negotiations of greater magnitude or complexity.

When an agreement is documented, each party must accept and acknowledge the agreement document. This can be done by applying digital confirmations like receipt of email or electronic signatures that do more than confirm but also instill in the agreement parties the agreement on the terms as read over. Best practices recommend storage in the clouds or project management platforms, whereby such documents can be shared, thus increasing accessibility and security.

Along with filing the actual agreement, post-negotiation follow-up plays a vital role in keeping the deal alive, as well as ensuring that all parties are on track as per the agreement. This follow-up may include scheduled check-ups and/or updates, which can be used to remind the parties involved of commitments and the problems that might arise. This initiative's governance builds and sustains the momentum of the agreement and maintains a strong professional alliance that shows that there is still a willingness to collaborate and achieve success.

To sum up, writing down their agreements is not only a matter of procedure, but it can be regarded as a strategic measure that helps to improve the efficiency and trustworthiness of professional negotiations. By clarifying and agreeing to what each side is committing to, written agreements propose the foundation for successful and lasting relationships.

Post-Negotiation Follow-Up

After a negotiation, it is time to roll up the sleeves and get down to the business of making the seeds of successful agreement take root and grow into a lasting partnership and concrete products. The post-negotiation process is not a mere administrative follow-up but an extension of the negotiation strategy as a whole to strengthen the agreement and also to maintain the commitment of all parties to the agreement. This stage is critical in averting the undermining of the deal or the feared silence that comes after a handshake deal, especially in the digital age.

There is also the danger of post-negotiation drift. Without prompt follow-up, deals can lapse, and feelings of excitement/relief that have characterized the end of the negotiation process can wear off. This is particularly so in online environments where physical evidence may be lost and, therefore, communication can become disjointed. As such, an effective follow-up plan is a requirement. The combination of follow-ups that constitute this plan needs to be made up of a set of professional, value-based follow-ups, which should not only be a restatement of terms agreed upon but also a follow-up that reiterates the strength of the partnership. As an example, a follow-up email could express gratitude towards the counterpart and describe the plan of action in the future: "Thanks to your cooperation- this is our agreed timeline and next actions." All of these communications will aid in keeping the lines of communication open and ensure that parties know what is expected of them as implementation progresses.

Management of delays and change of scope is yet another vital element in post-agreement management. Delays may happen because of unpredictable situations, and it is essential to counteract them in advance. Scripts of gentle nudges and renewed commitments can be very useful in this case. As an example, a routine email at the right time may say, "Just checking in as promised to see whether you require any assistance as we establish implementation." This not only acts as a reminder but also defines goodwill and the willingness to assist the counterpart towards the attainment of mutual interests.

The follow-up phase can be used in cases where unforeseen problems occur, like a partner developing cold feet or asking to rework some minor details, but not outweighing the whole agreement. Being flexible and long-term oriented when facing such situations can turn into a way of showing dedication and adaptation.

In addition to this, follow-up does not only assume upholding the existing contract but also building grounds for possible futures. An effective follow-up can open the possibility of referrals or repeat transactions, as an indication of trustworthiness and a desire for all parties to win. An example of what a successful follow-up session has resulted in, namely a referral, can demonstrate the wider usefulness of such a practice.

Lastly, it is imperative to have a proper debrief to learn and develop. The checklist on the rapid debrief may consist of a 10-minute list that will help to record what went right, what was unexpected, and what can be corrected. This reflection will not only aid in enhancing the skill of negotiation but also form a reservoir of experience that can form the basis of future negotiation tactics. Keeping a journal or an electronic log of such thoughts can offer long-term insights and assist a negotiator in monitoring their development and adjusting their approach to the changing demands.

Rapid Debrief Framework

The nature of a great negotiation is not just in the final result, but rather in the learning process it is able to generate. A debrief process that is neatly structured and time-efficient can go a long way toward sharpening negotiation skills. This framework promotes reflective practice that would help ensure there is a continual improvement in the skills of negotiation and mastery of negotiation.

Sitting at the centre of this framework is the 10-minute debrief checklist, which is designed to draw out the highlights of the negotiation experience in a rapid manner. This checklist helps the parties of the negotiation examine what was done better, what came as surprises, and what might be improved. By reflectively comparing these aspects on a regular basis, negotiators will be able to come up with valuable lessons that are useful in their progress pathways.

The debrief includes an important element: self-assessment with the help of specific questions. These questions are designed to get one to think in great depth, such as what signals did I miss? What was I least prepared to ERITHERE from? This self-observation will help identify trends, both positive and negative, and provide the areas of concentrated growth and development.

Besides that, it is recommended to keep a negotiation journal or a digital record. This log will act both as a source of experience and as a record of the details of each negotiation. It provides substantial measurements of progress over time in terms of trends and growth patterns. Lessons learned are not only encouraged to be shared among peers or mentors, but also the culture of accountability and diverse views is promoted.

In order to institutionalise this reflective practice, the framework recommends establishing regular peer debrief sessions, whether on a monthly or quarterly basis. Such meetings offer an avenue through which collaborative learning can take place since negotiators are capable of sharing information, questioning beliefs, and collectively advancing their negotiation skills.

The framework further identifies the need to note the development of the negotiation via an outcome log. Such a log, arranged according to the header row including the date, the context, the goal, the outcome, and what went and did not work, becomes an invaluable tool. Not only does it chronicle each negotiation, but it also guides a thorough self-assessment of key negotiating skills, including preparation, communication, creativity, closing, follow-up, and more.

Recording these insights makes negotiators better positioned to identify what is good and what is not. This awareness also allows them to reconsider their strategies and establish knowledgeable objectives to follow in future negotiations. Regular milestone checks can be done to have fun with positive progress and adjust goals, keeping an eye on continuous development.

In a nutshell, the Rapid Debrief Framework empowers every negotiation as a learning experience. It fosters a philosophy of self-enhancement, which will make the negotiators not just part of a transactional process but also develop craft masters. The given framework is evidence of how reflective intelligence can help considerably improve the speed of skill acquisition and, as a result, enable negotiators to become more active and skillful in their work.

Chapter 13: Tracking Growth and Mastery

Outcome Logs

In negotiation, it is key to continuous progress and perfection to develop a more systematic protocol. of consideration of your results in order to optimize past performance. The creation of a methodical outcome log will not only act as a record of past negotiation experiences. Still, it will also offer a key instrument of introspection and step-centered strategic development. This method assumes that each negotiation should be documented in terms of date, circumstances involved, aims/purposes, and results, with a frank evaluation of which tactics worked and which ones did not. This complete documentation of negotiation is in itself a clear roadmap of the path traversed in the negotiation that displays the patterns in performance and areas of development.

Outcome log qualifies as a self-feedback program with its analysis providing insights that are priceless in the development of negotiation abilities. By cataloging the experiences systematically, a trend will be seen in how they approach it, that is, either they are always well prepared or much more hesitancy is encountered in the closing stages. It is important to keep in mind that this self-awareness helps to identify strengths and weaknesses, both of which enable the negotiators to focus their studying and training activities.

Additionally, self-assessment rubrics, placed in these logs, may help to manage a formative examination of such fundamental skills as preparation, communication, creativity, and follow-up. Self-rating on these dimensions promotes and facilitates the development of a growth mindset, which is essential to negotiation success. These logs, used over time, become a history of how one is making progress and thus become an incentive and a source of accomplishment.

They should periodically review the outcome logs and re-adjust the targets and reward success. Whether quarterly or annually, these milestone reviews provide a chance to consider the growth, make changes in the strategy, and set new goals. They promote the initiative in personal growth, and this helps to make sure that negotiators always stay in line with their departing professional goals.

Also, discussing the lessons learned in outcome logs with peers or mentors can create accountability and help them acquire new sets of wisdom. The interactions involved in engaging in such dialogues not only reinforce learning but also build a community of practice in which shared experience and advice can contribute to improvement in general.

Adding outcome logs to the negotiation toolkit is a tactical act that leads to a masterful level. They can be used as a basis to create a strong, personal approach to negotiation, informed by real-life experience and checking practice. The documentation and review process is also a continuous process, which not only hastens learning but also makes confidence firmer. Therefore, the negotiator is able to negotiate or act swiftly and confidently in tricky situations and complex negotiations.

Finally, the necessity to go through outcomes logs is indicative of the effectiveness of reflection as a negotiation skill. It is with this perspective of constant learning and adjustment that negotiators can actually empower their requests, and each experience can be seen as an occasion of learning and success. The decision to codify and strategize on previous negotiations is not a form of record-keeping but a much-needed exercise in achieving excellence in negotiations.

Self-Assessment Rubrics

Self-assessment rubrics are valuable descriptions of how to improve self-development and practice negotiation skills. These rubrics are set up to give a systematic framework that will help the individual to rate their performance in different dimensions of negotiations. In exercising such reflective practice, strengths and areas of concern can be recognized to enable one to devise more effective negotiation strategies.

The self-assessment routine starts with a clear vision of the main capabilities of a successful negotiator. These generally involve preparing, communicating, creativity, closing, and follow-up. Each of those skills can be broken down into specific behaviors and actions that lead to effective results in negotiation. An example is that the preparation comes with extensive research and knowledge of the needs and goals of both parties. Communication should involve active listening and clear expression of views, whereas creativity includes the generation of creative solutions to obstacles that may emerge. Closure is about finalizing the deal properly, and follow-up is the aspect of making agreements go through and sustaining relationships.

In order to use self-assessment rubrics, people have to be able to rate themselves on each of the following core skills. This rating does not involve just a simple number but a qualitative assessment that takes into account some of the past negotiation points of illustrations. The recordings of such experiences will ultimately help negotiators pinpoint effective courses of action taken and those that failed, thus providing them with lessons that will help them shape their style and their effectiveness in negotiations. This self-introspection is key in the identification of patterns in the behavior that would either help in or hinder effective negotiation.

Further, self-assessment rubrics are motivating in nature because they invite cumulative reflection and advancement by establishing the habit of an outcome log. This is a chronological version of every negotiation with the date, context, goal, its result, what has been successful, what has not been, and the further steps. Documentation of this type is also imperative in measuring the progress over time and identifying common trends in the performance of a negotiation. Analyzing these logs after an interval of time, individuals will be able to appreciate their success and reconsider their targets to ensure that they always improve their thinking in terms of negotiation.

Another important factor in the implementation of a self-assessment rubric is the milestone review. Periodic reviews of this type offer a time to take stock. This can be done on a quarterly or yearly basis. These reviews allow the negotiators to re-evaluate their aims and objectives and change almost in line with their skills and experience development. Not only is this a way of bringing up areas of success, but it also presents a way to bring out the possible blind spots that might need further attention and advancement.

Ultimately, self-assessment rubrics will enable negotiators to assume control of their own individual and professional growth. Developing a culture of self-reviewing and constant improvement, these rubrics guarantee that a person will feel well-prepared to find their way in the world of negotiation with confidence and competence. When negotiators learn how to assess performance more accurately and how they can improve it, they become better equipped to record positive results and investment into long-term relationships in their work-related undertakings.

Milestone Reviews

Following up to determine progress is one of the core requirements of effective negotiation practices. These reviews can be known as milestone reviews, and they are critical checkpoints that people use to assess whether they are on track, realigning strategies, and celebrating along the way.

They do not just involve box-ticking but also form part of keeping pace and ensuring that targets are in line with other expectations.

Milestone reviews are built into the time to take a pause in a negotiation or a series of negotiations and reconsider the path taken. They give a rational plan to assess what has been done and what requires attention. This consideration is paramount to the identification of where improvement must also occur. In this manner, negotiators will be able to coordinate their efforts and resources towards attaining the best results.

Such reviews are especially useful whenever there is a series of phases or stages to a negotiation process. They also assist in the process of dissecting every stage, analyzing the dynamics involved, and perfecting tactics. For example, when reviewing quarterly intervals, one might discover that particular strategies are currently performing better than others, and therefore new priorities are enacted.

In addition, milestone reviews will create a culture of perpetual improvement. They urge negotiators to write about their experiences and how to learn from successes and failures, and use the information in a future negotiation. This paperwork may be in the form of negotiation diaries or electronic notebooks, all of which become very useful as they help individuals develop in both personal and professional aspects. A historical study of the past negotiations allows for the analysis of patterns and trends in how the process works to determine the trends that may come up in the future.

Reviewing the milestones can also be used to fuel team dynamics and collaboration in addition to individual development. Conducted in a team, these reviews will encourage free discussions and collective learning. The team members will be able to discuss personal experiences, share knowledge, and collectively brainstorm on how to overcome some of the challenges. Not only does this team approach enhance cohesion among the team members, but it is also able to pool the various minds, hence coming up with more innovative and effective negotiating approaches.

In addition, milestone reviews can serve as a motivational process. Rewarding or praising good behaviors, even the minor ones, encourages more effort in seeking to achieve more success. The morale of negotiators is boosted when they realize the effort and diligence that go into achieving a milestone, and it motivates them to meet future challenges with greater zeal.

To ensure that as many benefits as possible can be reaped out of milestone reviews, an arranged and systematic process should be established. This could include defining goals of the review meetings, creating supporting information and knowledge, and open and candid conversations. By naming expectations and objectives in each review, negotiators will be able to make sure such periods are effective and target-oriented.

Finally, milestone reviews are an excellent tool for achieving success in the negotiation. They offer a structure of monitoring and adaptation in which structures of negotiation flows remain deft and adaptive in the changing situations.

Through this practice, individuals and teams should be able to strengthen their negotiating ability, realize their point more efficiently, and develop long-term dependence founded on trust and mutualism. This means that the milestone review does not represent any mere formality but a strategic resource that can help negotiators reach their full potential.

Toolkit Refinement

In the constantly changing environment of a negotiation, honing the tool kit is similar to polishing a worn-down object to keep it sharp, sensitive to the overall demands of the interaction, and able to remain relevant to those demands. This carefully selected package of negotiation toolkits provides professionals with the framework around which they can develop flexible and powerful strategies to address the subtle needs of different negotiation situations.

This process starts with the acknowledgement that negotiation is a different thing in nature. This can be no truer than in negotiating salary, negotiating vendor contracts, and negotiating those complexities of remote work arrangements, each of which has different nuances requiring different approaches. The toolkit, therefore, has to be calibrated with perfection with particular circumstances grouping tools. It can also consist of generating up-to-date cheatsheets, including the above-mentioned Salary Negotiation Checklist, a Remote Meeting Script Bank, and others, which will always be helpful during critical areas of negotiation.

These tools must be constantly improved. Following every negotiation process, professionals must enter the process of reflective practice to analyze successful strategies and areas that still need improvement. This iterative process, in addition to strengthening the current set of tools, will prompt the introduction of new tools, helping to ensure that the toolkit can be used to keep up with the professional and changing environment in their industry.

In addition, the incorporation of digital devices into the negotiation toolbox can play a very important role in increasing its usefulness. Templates, scripts, and checklists can be saved on the computer and can be easily modified and amended. Such digital flexibility means no professional with a digital tool kit can ever be left without it, regardless of whether they are emailing, attending a virtual meeting, or seeing a colleague or client in real life.

The elements that should be present in the toolkit that would enable preparation and confidence must also be included. Creation of a series of pre-negotiation rituals, e.g., a checklist or breathing, may help in shifting nervous energy into a positive bargaining power, preparing the negotiator to get into high-stakes bargaining. Also, writing a confidence script to read prior to initiating the negotiation process can aid in building a positive attitude and attention span.

The promotion of cooperation and feedback is another important element of the toolkit's perfection. Sharing a toolkit with colleagues or mentors will help professionals receive suggestions and ideas on how to improve the toolkit. Other than increasing the power of individual tools, the collaborative design also creates a culture of lifelong learning and adjustment in teams or organizations.

The result of an expertly developed set of negotiation tools is that it gives the professional confidence and some modicum of flexibility when engaging in any form of negotiation in the professional workplace. It has the benefit of a versatile, yet systematic structure that can be adapted to the specific requirements of every negotiation situation, such that the practitioner is prepared to achieve optimal results and remain on amicable footing with their negotiating parties. Negotiators can invest in continuously bettering their arsenal, and in doing so, they can turn every negotiation into a growth experience where they succeed.

Chapter 14: Conclusion and Call to Action

Reinforcing the Mission

The communication aspect of the mission becomes one of the most important elements in the context of negotiation, and it goes beyond constant transactional negotiations. It corresponds to an even stronger desire to commit to ordering all actions and choices according to the radionuclide that lies behind the choice of negotiation procedure. This alignment does not just relate to following a list of predetermined targets but to following a philosophy that dictates every action taken along the path to an effective result.

The core idea of strengthening the mission is to acknowledge the fact that negotiation is a versatile process that undergoes dynamic changes. It demands an ongoing reassessment of strategies and approaches to make sure that they are contemporary and useful. This means a tight process of contemplating and evolving that urges negotiators to occasionally assess milestones, be jubilant in successes, and reassess their objectives. These periodic reviews are critical because they offer a platform to evaluate what has been achieved so far, where the negotiators need to improve, and propose new standards that need to be achieved in the future.

Negotiation is a multi-faceted mission, one that cannot be locked to a given set of parameters every single time. It requires an open mind; one that is ready to change and even adopt new strategies capable of furthering the overall objectives. This versatility is essential in an environment where the variables keep opening up, and the ability to adjust and change tack is a beneficial asset.

Further, it is important to develop a toolkit that is extensive and flexible to support the mission. This toolkit does not just represent a set of scripts and templates but is an evolving document as each negotiation experience takes place. It consists of a library of lessons learned, strategies of best practices, and new approaches that could be utilized in future scenarios. The toolkit is to be highly individualized to make it resonate with each negotiator, enable them to address the specific challenges that they encounter, and thus definitely empower them.

Another important step in strengthening the mission is sharing the toolkit with peers and gathering feedback from them. It helps to create a culture of cooperation and constant improvement, in which negotiators can learn and adapt their strategies or techniques based on each other's experiences. This shared expertise makes the toolkit more effective and ensures that it will not lose its relevance and strength.

Moreover, as a part of reinforcing the mission, I also need to celebrate success and to recognize the path that each negotiator goes through. It is about awareness of the fight and determination needed to step into practical situations, mental practices, and examine self-development. This is the celebration of progress, not only in terms of the final product but in the step-by-step advances made towards perfection.

The final step in mission reinforcement is to empower negotiators to put knowledge to practical use, or what they have learned into action, on the spot. It is to motivate them and to provide an incentive to them to continue to make decisions and to use new strategies or scripts in their next negotiation, and to have them see, feel, and experience that difference as a result of those small but meaningful steps. The fact of such direct application supports the very essence of the mission: negotiation is trainable, and every step that negotiators perform brings them closer to success.

Encouraging the mission boils down to inculcating the mentality of learning throughout life, in such a way that each negotiation is a chance to learn, to improve, and to become an even better negotiator. It is about an awareness that with every negotiation, there is the possibility of success that is within sight, and through empowering their ask, negotiators can deliver outcomes that are not only favourable but transformational.

Core Lessons Recap

In the book, the fundamental lessons lead to the entirety of the means of assimilating the art of negotiation. The critical aspect that is spotlighted concerns the change of conceptions that switch between a formidable challenge of negotiation and seeing it as an opportunity for value creation. This is a fundamental change, which makes negotiators adopt a positive disposition when discussing matters and aim to realize mutual win-win situations instead of having to win and the other one to lose. Preparation becomes one of the key strategies that diminishes the importance of rushing into any form of negotiation. This involves appreciating one's ambitions as well as those of the other party, as well as possible requirements and limitations. This kind of preparation gives the negotiators more power and flexibility in successfully going through conversations.

Micro-skills of communication are emphasized as the paraphernalia of the negotiator. Active listening skills, how to frame conversations, and the use of persuasive language come in handy to keep control and guide a conversation in the desired direction. Such skills are critical in overcoming objections and reframing discussions in order to brainstorm possible solutions. The book also examines scenario-based scripting where readers are presented with very practical templates applicable in different types of negotiating situations, such as salary negotiations, a contract between a vendor and the party, etc. These scripts come in handy and act as guidelines to the negotiators who can give a clear expression of their positions and effectively respond to counteroffers and counterarguments.

Use of psychological techniques complements the strategies used in negotiations, as negotiators can track and use the telltale signs. Strategies that include anchoring and framing are described, and their subtle ability to establish a mood as well as a limit of a negotiation is explained. The digital and cross-cultural issue of negotiation is also addressed, and it is noted that the field is changing rapidly, with both technology and international interactions becoming the most important parts of it. Negotiators are advised to follow these shifts, applying the digital space to research and showing cultural sensitivity to eliminate any wrongful interpretations.

Value creation is something repeated several times, underlying the fact that successful negotiations lead not only to an agreement, but to creating better relationships and to the possibility of further cooperation. The establishment of relations based on trust and ethical leverage, due to the lack of aggression, is also shown as a sustainable strategy. This will include preparation of the long-term advantages of negotiations and inculcating goodwill that goes beyond immediate profit.

There is no uniform pattern of growth, with continuous growth practices being encouraged, where the reader is provided with the impetus to treat negotiation as a skill built over time through practice and reflection. The book recommends having a negotiation journal where experiences can be documented and aid in the identification of patterns, learning experiences, and improvement of strategies. This way, negotiators will be able to monitor their performance, reward successes, and improve on weak areas.

Each lesson aims at enforcing the point that negotiation is not innate, but rather it is a kind of dynamic skill which can be learned by everybody who takes his/her time and effort to learn it. The conclusion of the book is the encouragement of readers to implement at least one new strategy into their next negotiation, as it is stated that small steps will ultimately get them a long way. With these lessons at the core, the book provides readers with the knowledge and tools that they will use to negotiate with confidence and the skills necessary to achieve desired outcomes as a result of an effective ability to ask.

Immediate Application

When it comes to negotiation, nothing can replace the direct implementation of negotiating tactics in order to turn intellectual learning into practical expertise. The following pages will discuss the essence of using negotiation tactics and features of performing in real-time, as well as the necessity of preparation and adaptability.

Look at the negotiation environment as a dynamic setting in which position strategies can be too stagnant to be effective. The effectiveness with which the learnt techniques are applied quickly can make profound changes in the negotiations. This flexibility needs a firm grounding of knowledge and advocacy to act on the deployment of tactics as the time may demand it. In intense circumstances, negotiators need more than the scripts they prepared; they should also be skilled enough to improvise them in line with the developing situation.

The secret to successful negotiation is preparation. More than simply understanding your objectives, it involves insight into what the other party wants, what his or her objections might be, and what is going on in the big picture. It is essential to plan all the possible ways and answers before proceeding to enter a negotiation. The foresight enables negotiators to switch easily when the negotiation turns in unforeseen directions.

During the negotiation process, micro-skills like active listening, re-framing, and strategic questioning can be used to redirect the conversations towards acceptable ends. Active listening not only entails listening but also making the necessary responses that are core to the needs and concerns of the other party. It opens up the path to more knowledgeable and compassionate reactions, which will open up opportunities to build bridges instead of causing conflict in any situation.

Another very important element is strategic questioning. Although asking specific questions, negotiators can find something more concealed, such as interests and motivation, which are impossible to notice at once. Not only does this trick provide valuable insights, but it also shows an actual interest in finding a mutually beneficial point of departure.

Reframing, on the other hand, is the action of re-contextualizing the conjecture. In cases of a stalemate, reframing allows the two parties to look at the issue in a new light, and there is a likelihood of another route being found to agreement. As an example, changing the cost-entered negotiation to a value creation-entered conversation may result in a doorway to creative solutions that please both sides.

The importance of digital tools regarding the immediacy of their application could hardly be exaggerated. Negotiators working in the modern, hybrid environment have to achieve proficiency in using technologies, such as Zoom or Slack, to keep things lively and explicated. The use of digital body language, including the use of direct eye contact using the camera, and well-spoken, precise words in chats, is an important element in avoiding lost or misunderstood messages.

Additionally, the psychological part of negotiation, such as how a person should manage his or her emotions and behave regarding the emotions of other people, is also essential. Knowing when to use a strategic pause, or refuse to allow a situation to be escalated to a higher authority, can spell the difference between a successful negotiation and a stalled one.

Last, immediate application does not end at the negotiation table. The second is post-negotiation, which is critical to follow-up orders to entrench agreements and avoid erosions of deals. This entails a wrap-up of the results, validation of the follow-ups, and keeping communication channels open. This level of conscientiousness not only helps the deal go through but also earns one's trust, creating the foundations of future negotiations.

In a nutshell, the direct use of negotiation techniques entails a complex process that involves preparation, flexibility, and sustained interactions. It is a way of making knowledge work by making every negotiation transaction not just a transaction, but a relationship-building process, which also leads to sustainable success.

Inspiring Lifelong Learning

Lifelong learning is all about constantly seeking knowledge due to curiosity and the need for personal and intellectual development. This voyage is not limited by the frames of formal education or the initial life period; on the contrary, it encompasses all life periods and dimensions. It is the process during which people strive to learn and know more about this world without refusing to accept new challenges and possibilities with an open mind and in a cheerful spirit.

At the centre of this method is the idea that learning is not only a tool to the goal but a goal itself. It is an attitude that values the experience of discovery and the pleasure of learning new things. Such a view changes the focus on the delivery of particular results to attachment to the experiences and development associated with every learning effort. By thinking this way, one develops the love of learning that is characteristic of one's/intellectual vitality in life.

In the fast-moving world, continuous learning skills are more important than ever before. The fast rate of technology development and the future of work necessitate that an individual be flexible and dynamic. Lifelong learning provides the necessary instruments that facilitate individual coping with the dynamic changes to retain relevance and competitiveness in the desired areas. It promotes the emergence of critical thinking and conflict-solving skills, which are needed to conquer the intricacies and ambiguities of the present age.

Further, through lifelong learning comes a feeling of enfranchisement and control. It enables individuals to become at the mercy of their own professional and personal growth and thus allows them to pursue what they love and enjoy with conviction. Since the philosophy emphasizes taking charge of the learning process, it allows a person to strive to explore other situations and opportunities, which expand the world and the range of experiences.

Inspiration for that lifelong learning, therefore, has to start early through establishing an atmosphere in which curiosity and experimentation are fostered. Schools, workplaces, and societies have a crucial role as learning places. These environments provide access to resources, support, and opportunities to grow, thus motivating an individual to learn outside of the traditional environments. The presence of technology can also contribute to the process of lifelong learning since it provides a variety of information and knowledge resources at the disposal of a learner.

Learner-friendly activities such as mentorship and collaboration also improve the lifelong learning process. Travelling with others who have the same interests as you or who are experienced in a specific area can offer plenty of ideas and inspiration. These interactions make a vibrant learning ecosystem, whereby knowledge is acquired and unique opinions are pursued. Collaboration processes not only enhance the personal learning processes but also act as a developmental resource to communities.

Finally, teaching about lifelong learning means instilling a long-term learning attitude of seeking challenge, change, and flexibility. It demands changes to be taken as a chance at growth and issues as a foster of learning. All this is achievable by embracing the attitudes mentioned and fostering personal potential, which can, in turn, lead to rich and meaningful lives through the acquisition of knowledge and understanding. Not only do these holistic methods of learning have great benefits for the individual, but they also hold massive advantages to society as a whole by way of innovation and taking steps towards a progressive future.

EPILOGUE

As we reach the culmination of our exploration into the dynamics of negotiation, it's essential to reflect on the transformative journey we've undertaken together. "Empower Your Ask" was designed not only as a manual of tactics but as a catalyst for change in how you perceive and engage in negotiations. The principles and strategies laid out were crafted to equip you with a robust toolkit, enabling you to navigate the complexities of modern negotiation landscapes with confidence and poise.

Throughout the chapters, we've delved into the nuances of mindset shifts, from overcoming the myth of the 'born negotiator' to embracing the learnable nature of negotiation skills. We've dissected the art of preparation, the power of communication micro-skills, and the strategic use of psychological tactics to reinforce your negotiating prowess. Each page aimed to demystify the negotiation process, offering clarity and actionable steps for achieving your goals.

The scenarios and scripts provided were not mere exercises but invitations to engage deeply with real-world challenges, fostering a sense of readiness and adaptability. By fostering a culture of continuous growth and reflection, this book encourages you to see each negotiation not as an isolated event but as a stepping stone towards mastery.

Your journey doesn't end here. The real value lies in applying these lessons, testing them in the varied terrains of your professional and personal lives. Whether you're negotiating a salary increase, sealing a business deal, or navigating the intricacies of a startup venture, remember that every negotiation is an opportunity to create value, build relationships, and drive success.

In the spirit of lifelong learning, I encourage you to revisit the strategies and tools shared within these pages, adapting them to new contexts and challenges. Share your stories, learn from your experiences, and inspire others with your successes. The potential for growth is limitless when you empower your ask with integrity and insight.

Thank you for embarking on this journey with a commitment to transform how you negotiate. Your dedication to mastering these skills ensures that you are not just a participant in negotiations but a leader, capable of shaping outcomes and influencing the world around you.

* 9 7 8 1 9 6 8 4 1 8 3 9 7 *